The Information Infrastructure

THE INFORMATION
INFRASTRUCTURE

A Harvard Business Review Paperback

Harvard Business Review paperback No. 90078

ISBN 0-87584-273-9

The *Harvard Business Review* articles in this collection are available individually, except "Target Information for Competitive Performance" by Robert E. Cole and "Jesse James at the Terminal" by William Atkins. Discounts apply to quantity purchases. For information and ordering contact Operations Department, Harvard Business School Publishing Division, Boston, MA 02163. Telephone: (617) 495-6192, 9 a.m. to 5 p.m. EST, Monday through Friday. Fax: (617) 495-6985, 24 hours a day.

© 1979, 1985, 1986, 1989, 1990, 1991 by the President and Fellows of Harvard College.

Editor's Note: Some articles in this book may have been written before authors and editors began to take into consideration the role of women in management. We hope the archaic usage representing all managers as male does not detract from the usefulness of the collection.

All rights reserved. No part of this book may be reproduced, stored in a retrieval system, or transmitted, in any form or by any means, electronic, mechanical, photocopying, recording, or otherwise without the prior written permission of the copyright holder.
Printed in the United States of America by Harvard University, Office of the University Publisher.
93 92 91   5 4 3 2 1

Contents

Information as a Competitive Weapon

Information Partnerships—Shared Data, Shared Scale
Benn R. Konsynski and F. Warren McFarlan
3

Information partnerships based on shared customer data can offer many benefits to the participants. Small companies can act big, reaching for markets formerly beyond their grasp, and big companies can act small, moving quickly and serving custom markets.

Rattling SABRE—New Ways to Compete on Information
Max D. Hopper
10

Proprietary information systems once conferred competitive advantage on their owners. That state of affairs may be fading as these systems become widely available. The source of advantage may be shifting from the characteristics of the system itself to the skill with which you use the system's output.

Reengineering Work: Don't Automate, Obliterate
Michael Hammer
18

Applying information systems to existing activities and routines may keep a company even with the competition. To take a quantum leap, however, a firm might better use the power of information technology to radically redesign the underlying processes.

Target Information for Competitive Performance
Robert E. Cole
27

Data can be had in overwhelming abundance from modern systems. But how much of the data stream produces useful information? A lot less than many American companies think, says the author of this article. Simpler, more selective systems provide better decision support.

The Case of the Soft Software Proposal
Thomas H. Davenport
37

At Middleton Mutual, the chief information officer is requesting $1 million to work on an expert system that supports underwriting. But does the proposed system add value to the basic business? How should this information-based proposal be evaluated when its benefits are largely intangible?

Information-Intensive Manufacturing

The Emerging Theory of Manufacturing
Peter F. Drucker
44

Separate strands of thought and action can be tied together to form a coherent theory of manufacturing. Central to the new theory is the recognition of what information means in manufacturing and how it ought to be used.

Postindustrial Manufacturing
Ramchandran Jaikumar
53

American companies have made huge investments in the information technology and machines that comprise flexible manufacturing systems (FMS). Unfortunately, the investments have often been squandered. Companies have misapplied the systems and have failed to cultivate the knowledge-based competencies that the systems require for efficient operation.

A CEO's Common Sense of CIM: An Interview with J. Tracy O'Rourke
Bernard Avishai
61

Establishing a computer-integrated manufacturing (CIM) facility is expensive and painful, but it may be the one way for some firms to justify staying in business. For the CEO of Allen-Bradley, the biggest obstacle in converting to CIM was the integration of the software driving the information system and the manufacturing control system.

Must CIM be Justified by Faith Alone?
Robert S. Kaplan
71

Investment in computer-integrated manufacturing (CIM) can be slowed or thwarted by knee-jerk financial analysis. An accurate assessment requires a sensible discount rate and careful estimates of tangible costs and benefits. But the key factor is the array of intangible benefits that CIM can yield.

Information and the Organization

The "Centrally Decentralized" IS Organization
Ernest M. von Simson
83

After a period of experimentation with decentralized information systems (IS) organizations, companies are again consolidating the function. This time, however, a balance is being struck that ensures genuine power sharing between IS managers and users.

Managing the Crises in Data Processing
Richard L. Nolan
87

Now over 10 years old, this classic article outlines the six stages of data processing systems development inside companies and the management implications. Using the benchmarks described in the article, managers can see where their organizations stand in the evolution of information gathering and processing.

Save Your Information System from the Experts
Richard S. Rubin
99

This succinct article makes a simple argument. If senior managers surrender information system decisions to technical experts, they are asking for big trouble. The author advocates an uncomplicated solution: an IS auditor.

Jesse James at the Terminal
William Atkins
103

As an organization becomes more dependent on its electronic information systems, it becomes more vulnerable to computer crime, especially by insiders. Using a single case study, the author develops some rules for crime prevention and damage control.

The Case of the Omniscient Organization
Gary T. Marx
109

To improve lagging productivity, a company put in place an extraordinary range of information systems to support its employees. The systems also allowed management to exert a high level of control over workers. Does the extension of authority through electronic means threaten the long-term health of the organization?

Information as a Competitive Weapon

How to gain another company's resources and customers – without having to own it.

Information Partnerships – Shared Data, Shared Scale

by Benn R. Konsynski and F. Warren McFarlan

Information technology empowers companies to compete, ironically, by allowing them new ways to cooperate. One of the most intriguing is the information partnership, facilitated by the sharing of customer data.

Perhaps the best way to illustrate the point is with a famous failure. Allegis Corporation was the brainchild of United Airlines management, which acquired the Hertz Corporation and Westin Hotels in the hope of creating an integrated travel company. The venture was quickly torpedoed by skepticism on Wall Street; nobody speaks of the Allegis Corporation today without adding the word fiasco. Yet in retrospect, it is hard to imagine a more prescient effort to form a market coalition to exploit what the new information technology has to offer – an opportunity for joint action that would have been completely impractical just a few years ago.

Look at Allegis from the travel customer's point of view. You rent a Hertz car and book reservations in a Westin hotel; you stay at Westin hotels and earn frequent flyer miles on United Airlines. The participant divisions share databases supported by powerful means to transmit, log, and retrieve information; and the company presents itself to the customer as a single source of travel services, incentives, and support. Eventually, one could imagine Allegis customizing travel programs for regular customers.

Allegis's hard lesson – and everybody else's excellent one – was that the partnerships engendered by information systems *need not be based on ownership*. Wall Street quite rightly reckoned that although United's top managers could develop synergies in servicing customers, they were not likely to enjoy any operational advantages. Indeed, would airline executives know how to grow the myriad businesses – car rental companies or hotels – that might have an interest in common data? The insurance industry, with many participants recovering from forays into the "financial supermarket," is learning this same lesson. Managers from companies in reciprocal industries should now be plotting common approaches to customers through relational databases, not plotting how to take each other over.

The really new opportunity, it turns out, is in joining forces *without* merging, the way American Airlines has allied with Citibank. In their arrangement, air mileage credit in the airline's frequent flyer program is awarded to credit card users – one mile for every dollar spent on the card. American has thus increased the loyalty of its customers, and the credit card company has gained access to a new and highly credit-worthy customer base for cross-marketing. This partnership has been expanded to include MCI,

---

Benn R. Konsynski is a visiting professor in the Information Systems Special Interest Group at the Harvard Business School. His last article in HBR (with James I. Cash, Jr.) was "IS Redraws Competitive Boundaries," March-April 1985. F. Warren McFarlan is the Ross Graham Walker Professor of Business Administration at the Harvard Business School. His last article in HBR (with William J. Bruns, Jr.) was "Information Technology Puts Power in Control Systems," September-October 1987.

a major long-distance phone company, which offers multiple airline frequent flyer miles for each dollar of long-distance billing. Recently, Citibank, the largest issuer of Visa and Mastercards, initiated a partnership to steer its 14.6 million Visa holders to MCI, a response to AT&T's entry into credit cards (the Universal card).

Through an information partnership, diverse companies can offer novel incentives and services or participate in joint marketing programs. They can take advantage of new channels of distribution or introduce operational efficiencies and revenue enhancements. Partnerships create opportunities for scale and cross-selling. They can make small companies look, feel, and act big, reaching for customers once beyond their grasp. Partnerships can make big companies look small and close, targeting and servicing custom markets. Partnerships, in short, provide a new basis for differentiation. We will be seeing many more of them.

The Virtues of Information Partnering

Market cooperation induces passing large volumes of electronic data precisely, instantaneously, and relatively cheaply. And not surprisingly, there have been dramatic improvements in the price and performance of systems delivering electronic databases and service to external parties over the past few years. New computer speeds and cheaper mass-storage devices mean that information can be archived, cross-correlated, and retrieved as never before—and in ways that may be customized for recipients. The widespread emergence of fiber-optic networks has greatly improved delivery to remote locations, in effect, at the speed of light.

Moreover, managers everywhere want to lessen their financial or technical exposure. Partnerships allow them to share investments in hardware and software—and the considerable expense of learning how to use both. The cost of developing certain configurations of software is particularly great, posing huge problems for small and midsize companies going up against big competitors. Realistically, software investments may be denominated in hundreds of millions of dollars, creating impenetrable entry barriers for smaller competitors—unless a number of them consolidate their purchasing power.

Likewise, the management of organizational learning, especially in our rapidly changing technical environment, is a mushrooming cost. While there is no shortcut to learning, information partnerships provide a way to reduce risks in leading-edge technology investments.

For the customer's part, the trend should only get stronger. Desktop clutter has led to a demand for simplification. Who wants 10 different terminals and 20 different software conventions on a single desk? Users want simple, user-friendly interfaces that enable them to reach out to a variety of services both within and without the company. This means they want companies to cooperate, at least on data interface

> **In an information partnership, you lessen your financial and technological exposure.**

standards. Users also have high service expectations, including faster response time, broader access to data files, and an increased desire for customized service. Partnerships help companies satisfy customers.

In response to these opportunities and ambient pressures, four different kinds of information partnerships have emerged: joint marketing partnerships, intraindustry partnerships, customer-supplier partnerships, and IT vendor-driven partnerships.

Joint Marketing Partnerships. Information technology offers companies an important new option: coordinate with rivals where there is an advantage in doing so and specialize where specialization continues to make sense.

The effort by IBM and Sears to market Prodigy is an example of such an effort. At an expense of more than $500 million, these companies have assembled a package of over 400 electronic data services—home banking, grocery shopping, restaurant reservations, and so on—to be delivered across a standard telephone network to millions of American homes. Individually, these services would be used so infrequently—and cost so much just to get hooked into—that customers would be unlikely to find any of them worthwhile. IBM and Sears have perceived that these services have considerable appeal when bundled together.

Again, travel companies are making use of electronic linkages to establish combined marketing programs—common customer databases, joint purchasing incentives—so that airlines, hotels, rental cars, and bank credit cards are all being woven into a single combined electronic marketing effort, spearheaded by such information networks as AMR's SABRE. The latter reaches into thousands of travel agencies and major companies, and all major U.S. airlines are involved with one partnering agreement or another.

In the airline industry, the scale needed to develop and manage a reservation system for travel agencies and individual clients is beyond the reach of the midsize airlines. Most of the latter have become clients of (and hostages to) the reservation information systems of the bigger carriers, such as SABRE. In Europe, two major coalitions have been created, the Amadeus Coalition and the Galileo Coalition; software for Amadeus is built around System One—which is the computer reservation system for Continental and Eastern—and Galileo is built around United's software.

Of course, there are only so many airlines, and the credit card industry is terribly fragmented. Banks that held back found themselves frozen out once the early movers had made their deals—more proof, if any more is needed, that our more dynamic competitive environment punishes procrastination as much as strategic blunders. More recently, marketing alliances have been formed among banks, grocery chains, and food companies.

In marketing partnerships, participant companies gain access both to new customers and territories and—like airline reservation systems—to economies of scale through cost sharing. For the provider of the data channel, sharing offers an opportunity to sell excess capacity in the channel, to ensure that the company's image and market position will not be compromised, and to extend a reach to customers once thought too expensive to reach. Need it be said that the customer's life, in turn, is greatly simplified?

And the path to a joint marketing program may be forged offensively or defensively. A market leader—for example, American Airlines—may seize the initiative and establish an imperative for participation, all the while controlling the partnership structure. On the other hand, Johnson & Johnson developed the COACT system, partially in response to concerns that previous initiatives by American Hospital Supply were hurting its sales. In another move, Texas Air acquired Eastern Airlines primarily to obtain its reservation system channel as a weapon to negate partially the impact United and American have had in the travel agencies.

Intraindustry Partnerships. The most obvious and potentially nettlesome information partnerships evolve not among companies offering complementary services but among small or midsize competitors who see an opportunity or a need to pool resources; they thus collect the capital and skills required to, in effect, create a new technology infrastructure for an entire industry. Think of the ATM banking networks.

In one case, 18 midsize paper companies jointly developed a global electronic information system to link themselves with hundreds of key customers and international sales offices. The system cost $50 million to develop, and it is meant to provide a speed and quality of response that would have been technically and financially unattainable by any of the individual participants acting in their own behalf.

These companies, whose sales amount to nearly $4 billion, came to feel that to compete effectively in a service-oriented business such as paper products, they had to provide on-line, global data interchange with key customers. They wanted to provide customers a virtually instantaneous means of placing status inquiries or new orders—in contrast with the 12 days that had become the industry norm. Moreover, considering their size, they were all uneasy about joining one of the proprietary information networks of their big, global competitors; they had seen what had happened to midsize airlines.

A group of hotels is now actively examining ways to set up a jointly owned hotel reservation system to deal with the high charges exacted by the airlines' systems. These hotels believe that as a group they bring enough critical mass to the market to warrant sharp reductions in charges per reservation.

Another coalition among competitors is the insurance value-added network services (IVANS), linking a roster of insurance companies to hundreds of home offices and thousands of independent agents. IVANS permits independent agents' offices all over the United States access to far-flung property and casualty insurance companies for policy issuance, price quotation, and other policy management services. It was initiated and created by the industry trade association, ACORD.

These forward-looking companies were concerned that several larger companies had invested in electronic channels of their own—and thus had the potential to monopolize the business of independent

> Companies that hold back forging a partnership may well find themselves frozen out by early movers.

agents. So the IVANS interface presents independent agents with a roster of smaller insurance companies and a level playing field—which benefits the agent, of course, who is concerned about maintaining the competitive environment ensured by multiple providers.

Understandably enough, a trade organization like ACORD will often be the fairest, hence most effective, broker in specifying development of a collaborative system among businesses. In the auto parts industry, MEMA/Transnet—connecting manufacturers and thousands of retailers—resulted from actions by the Motor and Equipment Manufacturers Association (MEMA).

At the extreme, an intraindustry partnership may be actively led by government. Consider the Tradenet System of Singapore, which manages the world's largest port. The Singapore government spent more than $50 million to link all brokers with relevant government agencies at the port—freight forwarders, shipping companies, banks, and insurance companies with customs officials and immigration officials. Clearing the port, which used to take a vessel two to four days, now takes as little as ten minutes. This startling reduction has halved the time any ship has to remain in port and is the key to ensuring that Singapore remains a port of choice in the Far East, where the competition is growing.

Customer-Supplier Partnerships. Some information partnerships take off from data networks set up by suppliers to service customers. Consider the program of Baxter Healthcare (formerly American Hospital Supply, which was purchased by Baxter Travenol), a major medical equipment and health care supplier. That company is now offering its customers (already connected to Baxter through AHS's direct electronic customer channel) office supplies and even the medical supplies of a competitor.

The system has created a platform, a single interface, for buyers to reach their many suppliers; participating supplier organizations now reach new customers at lower costs. For its part, Baxter has developed a major new revenue stream, offering a package of multivendor services. Since its introduction, the system has been in a constant state of reconfiguration and redevelopment—and to some extent, so have the participant companies. The system has prompted a new dynamism.

A retail grocery chain has renegotiated its relationship with a supplier of diapers, one of its high-turn items. Under the new partnership agreement, when a shipment of diapers leaves the retailer's warehouse, notice is sent to the manufacturer. No order is transmitted, no delivery schedule is requested; the manufacturer has a performance contract to make sure that the pipeline is full. This partnership is meant not merely to reduce inventories in the retailer's warehouse. Its intent is full-scale coordination: paperwork is significantly reduced on both sides (orders, quotes, complicated billing, and so on), production schedules are more responsive, and the two companies can trim their operations.

But sometimes suppliers and customers are so fragmented that neither side has the vision or resources to put together any kind of system—not until a third party takes the bull by the horns. Look at the American Gem Market System. Put together by a third party, one independently financed for this purpose, American Gem Market System has linked dozens of gem suppliers with hundreds of jewelry stores, replacing what had been a complex interpersonal network. Now gems are traded between partners who may not have personal knowledge of one another, but who trust the network provider.

IT Vendor-Driven Partnerships. A technology vendor may bring its technology to a new market and provide a platform for uninitiated industry participants to offer novel customer services. General Electric Information Services and Automatic Data Processing provide just such data-interchange platforms. When propitious, information companies become the strategic linchpin for new business organization.

Take the case of ESAB, a large European welding-supplies and equipment company, which tripled in size between 1973 and 1987 – a time when sales halved in the industry as a whole. The key to that company's growth has been an alliance with a large independent network vendor. It used that third party's information services to facilitate acquiring and rationalizing failing companies all over Europe: closing their plants, moving production of what had been local brands to a central plant, while providing old customers an on-line order-entry service. ESAB did not have the resources in-house to build such a Europeanwide system.

From the customers' point of view, the local offices of the old companies still provided goods and services. In fact, the information system governed the

> **Partnership is strategy. It will fail without the stubborn vision of the companies' strategic planners.**

company's production schedule, manufacturing, and shipping so that customers got products, usually overnight, without realizing they were no longer dealing with a local manufacturer. This strategy has slashed costs dramatically. ESAB has, in effect, replaced inventory and plant with information.

Moreover, an information vendor may form a research alliance with a major customer. Some establish joint information research projects through beta sites – where a manufacturer tests a new technology with selected clients to debug it or understand more fully how it may be used. Such coalitions provide advantages to both parties. Vendors gain valuable insight into the practical field problems associated with their technology. Their ability to resolve their customers' problems, especially the problems of prestige accounts, gives vendors' sales forces highly visible references for further promotion. The customer learns about and participates in a new technology that may otherwise be beyond its skill and financial resources.

Laying the Foundation

Partnership is strategy. A manager must continue to ask: What lines of business should I provide exclusively, and how can I leverage them through partnering? What are the appropriate adjunct services that will drive my products to new markets? Where can I profitably offer joint purchasing incentives without confusing or eroding my existing customer base?

Naturally, partnerships can fail either because of overly optimistic assessments of the benefits or inadequate attention to the difficult challenges of administering the relationship. No single formula will ensure successful partnerships, but our research has identified some of their main supports. Most successful partnerships have:

Shared Vision at the Top. It may seem a cliché by now, but there are really no substitutes for champions in senior management. If a partnership is to overcome the inevitable divergences of interest among companies, top executives have to share an understanding of the specific benefits of collaboration – cost reductions, new customers, cross-selling. Partnering, again, is a strategic matter that needs the stubborn vision of the companies' strategists. The airlines and credit card companies came to agreement because their CEOs hammered out details in face-to-face discussions. Neither side was looking for a quick killing.

Reciprocal Skills in Information Technology. Competence in such areas as telecommunications, database design, and programming must be reasonably sophisticated in all partners – and at a very high level in the partner that is playing a leadership role in developing the information platform. Minimally, all participant companies should be able to manage telecommunications networks, have very high standards of internal quality control, at least with respect to data handling, and be accustomed to working with very large databases. Many companies that have initiated electronic data-interchange agreements have been shocked to find partners unable to assimilate even modest data technologies and applications.

Concrete Plans for an Early Success. Partnerships grow from strength to strength. It is important to plan introduction of the system so that people across participant companies can experience positive results at the start. Early successes—such as pilot installations in key regions—create a sense of accomplishment and commitment.

Usually, partners will have to go some lengths to test their hardware and software and to ensure that their general direction is technically feasible. They should *not* settle for the lowest common denominator; rather, the more competent side must assist in upgrading the technical or business environment of its partner.

Persistence in the Development of Usable Information. Mere ownership of a database—say, of a company's current customers—is no guarantee that information is organized in a form that can pass beyond corporate boundaries to partners. In fact, the most expensive and time-consuming prelude to partnership is organization of cost-effective data transmission.

You have to send information in a way that is useful to others without compromising the confidentiality of your company's secrets. Information has to be packaged for all partners by all partners, which requires the joint design of data definitions, formats, relationships, and search patterns.

Coordination on Business Policy. Partnering means more than sharing data. Companies share applications that involve a considerable degree of integration across company lines. So not only will a joint team be needed to develop the initial system but an ongoing task force will also be needed to guide its evolution. Partners must involve themselves in such mundane tasks as defining common procedures and common standards of systems development and maintenance. They'll have to develop common codes for products, customers, and data communications. Partners also need articulated procedures for surfacing conflicts, addressing per-

> **Companies that share software applications are in for a considerable degree of integration.**

ceived injustices, and rethinking the terms of the partnership.

One recent partnership we tracked verged on collapse because the receiving partner had not brought its business systems into line with its partner's. It first had to print out incoming documents and then manually recode and rekey the information so as to be compatible with its own database architecture.

Appropriate Business Architecture. Partnering companies have to establish the structures and guidelines that ensure fairness and profit. This means agreeing on rules that constitute equal treatment under the system. It also means addressing possible asymmetries in their underlying interests—making sure the deal is structured so that partners contribute what they can really afford to and so that they will profit from the system in proportion to what they put in.

In the airline industry, the issue of screen bias—where competing airlines' flights are shown below those of the lead partner—has been as explosive as exorbitant charging. Additionally, some airlines have contended that AMR and United have examined the booking data of other partners to gain better insight into competitive market positioning, while denying

---

Four Questions for the General Manager

1. *Is your company vulnerable to new information partnering, and are there ways to forge alliances of your own to preempt them?* In reality, alliances mean many more losers than winners, since early movers either freeze others out of the game or build economies of scale that become hard to replicate. Timing is crucial. True, if you start too early, you and your partners may get into technical trouble or face a market that doesn't know it wants your product. But start too late, and the window of opportunity will be closed.

2. *Does your business strategy realistically assess the implications of the transfer of power and authority to partners?* False steps can be extraordinarily expensive and time-consuming to undo.

3. *Are your potential partners financially viable, and do they represent the right collection of players for potential synergy?* In selecting this particular set of partners, have you broadly analyzed the set of future options that you may be foreclosing? Today's short-term opportunity may be tomorrow's strategic liability.

4. *Is the technical infrastructure you have in place the right one to effect and manage the kinds of strategic alliances that you are considering?* Are you overreaching your skills or contemplating an approach that does not use your most accessible technical capabilities?

access to this data to others. AMR and United have, naturally, denied the charge.

Or take the case of the small, startup book distribution company that approached a big retailer with the idea of using the retailer's sales data to identify a customer's potential interest in books. The book distributor would, for example, promote books about gardening to recent purchasers of gardening tools. However, examination of the retailer's sales data revealed that the two companies would have had to integrate 11 different databases to accomplish the task of the joint venture – too expensive and risky for the undercapitalized book distributor.

In the past, much of the thinking about and research on IT applications has focused on how the individual company can manage its information system assets. This has led to intense discussion of the general manager's role (see the insert, "Four Questions for the General Manager"), deployment of IT resources inside the company, and the structure and nature of appropriate planning and control systems. More recently, extensive work has been done to develop interorganizational system links between a company and its customers and suppliers.

Today, however, the opportunities have broadened, and senior managers are discussing the establishment of strategic information partnerships with other companies – within their industry and without. In tomorrow's business environment, many more companies will hit upon the imperatives of developing collaborative IT relationships. The question is whether they will do so playing offense or defense – or, indeed, if they will even be able to get their hands on the ball.

Reprint 90506

"I can assure you, Merkins, that my mind is not under the control of space aliens, but I appreciate your concern."

Lessons for survival in the era of the "information utility."

Rattling SABRE – New Ways to Compete on Information

by Max D. Hopper

I have built my career, and American Airlines has built much of its business, around massive, centralized, proprietary computer systems. Developing these systems consumed millions of man-hours and billions of dollars, but their marketplace advantages were huge. As a result, our experience underscored the competitive and organizational potential of information technology. At the risk of sounding immodest, we helped define an era.

That era is over. We are entering a new era, one in which the thinking that guided "best practice" as recently as five years ago is actually counterproductive. In this new era, information technology will be at once more pervasive and less potent—table stakes for competition, but no trump card for competitive success. As astute managers maneuver against rivals, they will focus less on being the first to build proprietary electronic tools than on being the best at using and improving generally available tools to enhance what their organizations already do well. Within their companies, they will focus less on developing stand-alone applications than on building electronic platforms that can transform their organizational structures and support new ways of making decisions.

Who, by now, cannot recite the computer-based success stories of the 1970s and 1980s?

☐ SABRE, American Airlines's reservation system, which eventually became a computerized reservation system (CRS), and Apollo, the other leading CRS, transformed marketing and distribution in the airline industry.
☐ American Hospital Supply's ASAP order-entry and inventory-control system generated huge sales increases for the company's medical products and turned it into an industry leader.
☐ United Service Automobile Association used its Automated Insurance Environment—a collection of

On its own, an information system can't build enduring business advantage.

telecommunication systems, databases, expert systems, and image-processing technologies—to consistently outperform its insurance industry rivals in service quality, premium growth, and profitability.

Max D. Hopper is senior vice president for information systems at American Airlines, a subsidiary of AMR Corporation, and vice chairman of AMR Information Services. He joined American in 1972 as director of SABRE, the airline's computerized reservation system.

☐ Mrs. Fields Cookies relied on its Retail Operations Intelligence system, an automated store management network, to build and operate a nationwide chain of 400 retail outlets without a costly and stifling headquarters bureaucracy.

These and a handful of other well-known computer systems (the Information Technology Hall of Fame, if you will) represent an important chapter in the application of electronic technologies to build competitive advantage and enhance organizational effectiveness. But it is time to turn the page. In 1984, F. Warren McFarlan published an influential article in HBR on the competitive potential of information technology.[1] He asked managers to consider how information systems might benefit their companies. Could the technology build barriers to competitive entry? Could it increase switching costs for customers? Could it change the balance of power in supplier relationships? He went on to argue that for many companies the answer was yes. By being the first to develop proprietary systems, pioneers could revolutionize their industries.

Increasingly, however, the answer is no. While it is more dangerous than ever to ignore the power of information technology, it is more dangerous still to believe that on its own, an information system can provide an enduring business advantage. The old models no longer apply.

The Information Utility

The new era is driven by the greatest upheaval in computer technology since the first wave of modern computer development 30 years ago. We are finally (and just barely) beginning to tap the real potential of computer functionality. As we change what computers can do, we must change what we do with computers.

Think of it as the emergence of an "information utility." Using superfast RISC architectures, hardware suppliers are delivering enormous processing power at remarkably low costs. UNIX and other software and communications standards are bringing unprecedented portability among different vendors' products and among different classes of products. Software tools like relational databases, expert systems, and computer-aided software engineering are helping create powerful applications that meet specialized needs at reasonable costs. The ultimate impact of these and other technical developments is to give end-users greater power to shape their computer systems and manage their information needs. Increasingly, technology is allowing groups and individuals within companies to perform many of the functions once reserved for data processing professionals.

It is hardly news to most managers that technology is changing faster than ever. Yet I wonder how many appreciate just how radical and rapid the changes are. Over the past two decades, price/performance ratios for computer technology improved at an annual compound rate of roughly 10%. In recent years, those

> **Soon computers will be as ubiquitous as telephones and as easy to use.**

ratios improved at a compound rate closer to 40%. This massive acceleration in performance will have profound implications for how computers are used and how useful computers are. Three features of the new environment will be particularly important.

Powerful workstations will be a ubiquitous presence in offices and factories, and organizations will use them far more intensively and creatively than they do today. One of the paradoxes of the information age is that computers become easier to use as they become more powerful and complex. That's what is so important about dramatic hardware advances like microprocessors with a million transistors on a chip. Personal workstations running at near supercomputer speeds will finally be powerful enough to be simple and thus truly useful. Meanwhile, new graphical user interfaces are creating screen environments (electronic desktops) that make it quicker for employees to become skilled with their workstations, to move between systems without extensive retraining, and to develop the confidence to push the functionality of their machines.

In the not-so-distant future, computers will be as familiar a part of the business environment as telephones are today. They will also be as simple to use as telephones, or at least nearly so. As a result, companies will find it harder to differentiate themselves simply by automating faster than the competition. It will be easier for every organization to automate and to capture the efficiency benefits of information technology. This leaves plenty of room for competitive differentiation, but differentiation of a new and more difficult sort.

Companies will be technology architects rather than systems builders, even for their most critical applications. The widespread adoption of standards and protocols in hardware, software, and telecommu-

---
1. F. Warren McFarlan, "Information Technology Changes the Way You Compete," HBR May-June 1984, p. 98.

nications will dramatically recast the technology-management function. At American Airlines, for example, we have spent 30 years handcrafting computer systems. We like to think we're better at this than most and that our skills in hardware evaluation, project management for software development, and systems integration have given us an important leg up on the competition. But we look forward to the day when we can buy more and more of our hardware and software from third-party vendors capable of tailoring their systems to our needs – and that day is rapidly approaching.

InterAAct, our major new initiative for organizational computing, is a good example. Unlike SABRE, which incorporates a vast amount of AMR-developed technology, InterAAct is built around hardware and software provided by third-party vendors: workstations from AT&T, IBM, and Tandy; minicomputers from Hewlett-Packard; HP's NewWave presentation software and Microsoft Windows; local area networks from Novell. We play a role in systems integration (in particular, merging the networks), but outside suppliers are capable of delivering more value than ever before.

Of course, if we can buy critical hardware and software from outside vendors, so can our competitors. Our skills as electronic-tool builders, honed over decades, will become less and less decisive to our information technology strategy. This may sound like bad news, but we welcome it. We're not in business to build computer systems; our job is to lead in applying technology to core business objectives. We don't much worry if the competition also has access to the technology; we think we can be smarter in how we use it.

Economies of scale will be more important than ever. We have entered the age of distributed computing, an age in which a young company like MIPS Computer Systems delivers a $5,000 workstation with processing speeds comparable to those of a $3 million IBM 3090 mainframe. Yet the amount of information required to solve important business problems also keeps growing, as does the capacity of telecommunications systems to transmit data quickly and reliably between distant locations. More than ever, then, the benefits of distributed computing will rely on access to vast amounts of data whose collection and storage will be managed on a centralized basis. The proliferation of desktop workstations will not erode the importance of scale economies in information processing.

Consider the airline industry. American Airlines began working on a computerized reservation system in the late 1950s as the volume of reservations began to outrun our capacity to handle them with index cards and blackboards. In 1963, the year SABRE debuted, it processed data related to 85,000 phone calls, 40,000 confirmed reservations, and 20,000 ticket sales. Today there are 45 *million* fares in the database, with up to 40 million changes entered every *month*. During peak usage, SABRE handles nearly 2,000 messages per *second* and creates more than 500,000 passenger name records every day. As we enhance SABRE, we are aggressively replacing "dumb terminals" in travel agents' offices, airline reservation offices, and airports with workstations capable of intensive local processing. But as a system, SABRE still works only in a centralized environment. The level of data collection and management it must perform dwarfs the demands of the 1960s just as thoroughly as the performance of today's computers dwarfs the performance of their ancestors.

The continued importance of scale economies has at least two major implications for information technology. First, truly useful computer systems are becoming too big and too expensive for any one company to build and own; joint ventures will become the rule rather than the exception. Second, organizations (like AMR) that have developed centralized systems will eagerly share access to, and sometimes control of, their systems. For companies to remain low-cost providers of information, they must tap the enormous capacities of their systems. Tapping that capacity requires opening the system to as many information suppliers as possible and offering it to as many information consumers as possible.

From Systems to Information

I do not mean to diminish the pivotal role of information technology in the future or to suggest that technology leadership will be less relevant to competitive success. Precisely because changes in information technology are becoming so rapid and unforgiving and the consequences of falling behind so irreversible, companies will either master and remaster the technology or die. Think of it as a technology treadmill: companies will have to run harder and harder just to stay in place.

But that's the point. Organizations that stay on the treadmill will be competing against others that have done the same thing. In this sense, the information utility will have a leveling effect. Developing an innovative new computer system will offer less decisive business advantages than before, and these advantages will be more fleeting and more expensive to maintain.

The role of information technology has always been to help organizations solve critical business problems or deliver new services by collecting data, turning data into information, and turning information into knowledge quickly enough to reflect the time value of knowledge. For 30 years, much of our money and energy has focused on the first stage of the process—building hardware, software, and networks powerful enough to generate useful data. That challenge is close to being solved; we have gotten our arms around the data-gathering conundrum.

The next stage, and the next arena for competitive differentiation, revolves around the intensification of analysis. Astute managers will shift their attention from *systems* to *information*. Think of the new challenge this way: In a competitive world where companies have access to the same data, who will excel at turning data into information and then analyzing the information quickly and intelligently enough to generate superior knowledge?

On Wall Street, there are stock traders who wear special glasses that allow for three-dimensional representations of data on their screens. They need three dimensions to evaluate previously unimaginable quantities of information and elaborate computer models of stock patterns. Manufacturers Hanover has developed an expert system to help its foreign-currency traders navigate through volatile markets.

In our industry, powerful new tools are helping us answer faster and more precisely questions we have struggled with for years. What is the best price to charge for each perishable commodity known as an airline seat? How do you reroute aircraft after a storm disrupts airport operations? How do you distribute your aircraft between airports? How do you meet the special needs of each passenger without pricing your basic service out of reach? As the process of analysis intensifies, decisions we once made monthly, we'll make weekly. Those we made weekly, we'll make daily. Those we made daily, we'll make hourly.

Consider yield management, the process of establishing different prices for seats on a flight and allocating seats to maximize revenues—that is, calculating the optimal revenue yield per seat, flight by flight. Yield management is certainly one of the most data-intensive aspects of the airline business. Computers review historical booking patterns to forecast demand for flights up to a year in advance of their departure, monitor bookings at regular intervals, compare our fares with competitors' fares, and otherwise assist dozens of pricing analysts and operations researchers. During routine periods, the system loads 200,000 new industry fares a day. In a "fare war" environment, that figure is closer to 1.5 million fares per day.

The initial challenge in yield management was to build software powerful enough to handle such demanding analyses. We spent millions of dollars developing SABRE's yield-management software, and we consider it the best in the world. Indeed, we believe our pricing and seat-allocation decisions generate hundreds of millions of dollars of incremental annual revenue. For years, we guarded that software jealously. Since 1986, however, we have sold SABRE's revenue-management expertise to any company that wanted to buy it. One of our subsidiaries—called AA Decision Technologies, many of whose members built our original yield-management applications—is

During a fare war, our yield-management system loads 1.5 million fares a day.

knocking on the doors of airlines, railroads, and other potential customers. Why? Because we believe our analysts are better at using the software than anyone else in the world. Whatever "market power" we might enjoy by keeping our software and expertise to ourselves is not as great as the revenue we can generate by selling it.

Similarly, Mrs. Fields has begun marketing to other retail chains the sophisticated networking and automation system with which it runs its cookie operations. Price Waterhouse is helping companies like Fox Photo evaluate and install the Retail Operations Intelligence system, the backbone of Mrs. Fields's nationwide expansion.

TICKETS COURTESY OF OMNI TRAVEL, CAMBRIDGE, MA

This is the competitive philosophy with which American Airlines is entering the new era: we want to compete on the use of electronic tools, not on their exclusive ownership.

Computers and Competition: SABRE Reconsidered

Perhaps no case study better illustrates the changing competitive role of computer technology than the evolution of the system that helped define the old era—SABRE. According to conventional wisdom on SABRE, the fact that American Airlines developed the world's leading computerized reservation system generated substantial increases in traffic for us by creating market-power advantages over the competition. This has always been a difficult proposition to document. Analysts once pointed to so-called "screen bias" as a source of marketing advantage, even though the government-mandated elimination of such biases in 1984 produced no appreciable decline in bookings for American Airlines. Others argued that American's access to CRS data regarding the booking patterns of travel agents gave us an incalculable information and marketing edge over our rivals—an argument that has proven groundless. Now the experts speak of a halo effect that by its very nature is impossible to identify or document.[2]

We are proud of what SABRE has achieved, and we recognize that it represents a billion-dollar asset to the corporation. But I have always felt the folklore surrounding SABRE far exceeded its actual business impact. SABRE's real importance to American Airlines was that it prevented an erosion of market share. American began marketing SABRE to travel agents only after United pulled out of an industry consortium established to explore developing a shared reservation system to be financed and used by carriers and travel retailers. The way American was positioned as an airline—we had no hubs, our routes were regulated, and we were essentially a long-haul carrier—meant that we would have lost market share in a biased reservation system controlled by a competitor. SABRE was less important to us as a biased distribution channel than as a vehicle to force neutral and comprehensive displays into the travel agency market.

My concerns about the conventional wisdom surrounding SABRE, however, go beyond the issue of market power. SABRE has evolved through four distinct stages over the past 30 years. In each stage, it has played different roles within American Airlines, and each role has had a different impact on the industry as a whole. Unfortunately, most analysts mistake the CRS distribution stage for the entire story. To do so is to invariably draw the wrong lessons.

SABRE took shape in response to American's inability to monitor our inventory of available seats manually and to attach passenger names to booked seats. So SABRE began as a relatively simple inventory-management tool, although by the standards of the early 1960s, it was a major technical achievement.

Over the years, the system's reach and functionality expanded greatly. By the mid-1970s, SABRE was much more than an inventory-control system. Its technology provided the base for generating flight plans for our aircraft, tracking spare parts, scheduling crews, and developing a range of decision-support systems for management. SABRE and its associated systems became the control center through which American Airlines functioned.

American installed its first SABRE terminal in a travel agency in 1976, inaugurating its now familiar role as a travel-industry distribution mechanism. Over the decade that followed, we added new services to the database (hotels, rail, rental cars), built powerful new features to help travel agents offer better service, increased the installed base of SABRE terminals, and created a training and support infrastructure. SABRE now operates in more than 14,500 subscriber locations in 45 countries. Largely as a result of the proliferation of such systems, travel agents now account for more than 80% of all passenger tickets as compared with less than 40% in 1976. SABRE and its CRS rivals truly did transform the marketing and distribution of airline services.

> A travel agent can replace SABRE in just 30 days—so how can SABRE create long-term competitive advantage?

Today, however, SABRE is neither a proprietary competitive weapon for American Airlines nor a general distribution system for the airline industry. It is an *electronic travel supermarket*, a computerized middleman linking suppliers of travel and related services (including Broadway shows, packaged tours, currency rates) to retailers like travel agents and directly to customers like corporate travel departments. Speak with any of the 1,800 employees of the SABRE Travel Information Network, the system's

---

2. For a comprehensive review of CRS technology in the airline industry, see Duncan G. Copeland and James L. McKenney, "Airline Reservation Systems: Lessons From History," *MIS Quarterly*, June 1988.

marketing arm, and you will hear that their division doesn't treat American Airlines materially differently from the other 650 airlines whose schedules and fares are in the system. American pays SABRE the same booking fees as other airlines do. SABRE's capacity to write tickets and issue boarding passes works similarly on other large carriers as it does on American flights. Although limited performance differences remain (largely as a result of SABRE's technical heritage as an in-house reservation system), SABRE programmers are working to overcome these limitations and put all carriers on an equal footing in the long term.

I don't deny that there is some halo effect from SABRE that benefits American Airlines in the marketplace, although we have never been able to determine the magnitude or causation. But the core identifiable benefit American Airlines now receives from SABRE is the revenue it generates. This is not an inconsequential advantage, to be sure, but it is difficult to argue that the SABRE system tilts the competitive playing field in ways that uniquely benefit American Airlines. This is not necessarily how we would prefer it, but it is what the technology, the market, and the U.S. government demand. There is no compelling reason for a travel agency to accept a CRS that does not provide the most comprehensive and unbiased system for sorting through thousands of potential schedules and fares. If SABRE doesn't do the job, another system will. SABRE's industry-leading U.S. market share of 40% means that rival systems account for three out of every five airline bookings.

I receive weekly reports on our "conversion wars" with Covia, whose Apollo reservation system remains our chief competitor, and the other U.S.-based CRS systems. Subject to contract-term limitations that are established by the U.S. government, it takes only 30 days for a travel agent who is unhappy with SABRE to pull the system out and install a competing system. If a CRS can be replaced within a month by a rival system, can it really be considered a source of enduring competitive advantage? The old interpretations of SABRE simply no longer apply.

As a group of HBR authors argued, "Early developers of single-source or biased sales channels should plan for the transition to unbiased electronic markets. That way, they can continue to derive revenues from the market-making activity."[3] The alternative,

3. Thomas W. Malone, JoAnne Yates, and Robert I. Benjamin, "The Logic of Electronic Markets," HBR May-June 1989, p. 168.

they might have added, is for the biased channel to disappear altogether in favor of unbiased markets offered by other suppliers.

This is the future of electronic distribution. It is increasingly difficult, if not downright impossible, for computerized distribution systems to bind customers to products. Smart customers simply refuse to fall into commodity traps. (Indeed, American Hospital Supply has opened ASAP to products from rival companies.) It is increasingly difficult to design information systems that locked-out competitors or coalitions of locked-out competitors can't eventually imitate or surpass. It is increasingly difficult for one company to marshal the financial resources to build

> We went it alone on SABRE. This time we're sharing ownership with Marriott, Hilton, and Budget Rent-A-Car.

new information systems on the necessary scale.

We are applying these new rules outside the airline realm. AMRIS, a subsidiary of AMR, is developing a computerized-reservation and yield-management system for the hotel and rental car industries. Its power and sophistication will exceed anything currently available. We expect that the introduction of the Confirm system, scheduled for 1991, will affect pricing strategies and marketing techniques in the hotel and rental car industries in much the way Apollo and SABRE transformed the airline business. But we are not approaching the system itself in the same way we approached SABRE – at least three major differences stand out.

For one, we are not going it alone. AMRIS has formed a joint venture with Marriott, Hilton, and Budget Rent-A-Car to develop and market the Confirm system. Moreover, there will be nothing biased about Confirm's reservation functions – no tilted screen displays, no special features for the sponsors. Finally, the management aspects of the system, such as the yield-management software, will be generally available to any hotel or rental car company that wants to buy them. Confirm's sponsors are participating in the creation of the most sophisticated software in the world for their industries; but the moment the system is operational, they will offer its tools to their competitors around the world.

Not all companies will benefit equally from this new system. As is true with marketing or finance or employee development, some organizations will excel in manipulating, analyzing, and responding to the data Confirm generates. But no company will be locked out of access to the data or the opportunity to use it to compete. As in airlines and so many other industries, competition shifts from building tools that collect data to using generally available tools to turning data into information and information into knowledge.

Building the Organizational Platform

As with competition between companies, technological change will have profound consequences for the role of computers within companies. Until recently, I was not a champion of office automation. Workstations were simply not powerful enough nor affordable enough nor easy enough to use nor capable enough of being integrated into networks to justify large investments in organizational computing. Indeed, a visitor to my office would be hard-pressed to find more than a handful of personal computers on the desks of the information technology professionals.

In the last few years, though, as a result of the technology changes I have outlined here, my caution has given way to genuine enthusiasm. But in this area too, it is time for new thinking. Understandably, given the earlier limitations of the technology, most companies approached office automation with an "applications" mind-set. They developed discrete systems to make administration more efficient, to improve planning and control, or to deliver particular services more effectively.

In the future, workstations will link every company location from Boston to Tulsa to Dallas.

We are taking a different approach. AMR has embarked on a multiyear, $150 million initiative to build an information technology platform modeled directly on the utility concept. This platform, called InterAAct, provides for the convergence of four critical technologies: data processing, office automation, personal computing, and networking. InterAAct will provide an intelligent workstation for every knowledge worker at AMR and will guarantee that every employee, no matter the rank or function, has easy access to a workstation. These workstations will be part of local area networks connecting work groups and a corporatewide network linking every location in the company, from departure gates in Boston to the underground SABRE facility in Tulsa, Oklahoma to the CEO's office in Dallas/Fort Worth.

The goal of InterAAct is *not* to develop stand-alone applications but to create a technology platform—an electronic nervous system—capable of supporting a vast array of applications, most of which we have not foreseen. InterAAct is an organizational resource that individuals and groups can use to build new systems and procedures to do their jobs smarter, better, and more creatively. It should eliminate bureaucratic obstacles and let people spend more time on real work—devising new ways to outmarket the competition, serve the customer better, and allocate resources more intelligently.

InterAAct began to take shape in 1987, and rollout started last June. It will take at least three years to extend the platform throughout the AMR organization. We are approaching the project with four guiding principles.

1. The platform must give each employee access to the entire system through a single workstation that is exceptionally easy to use and that operates with a standard user interface throughout the company.

2. The platform must be comprehensive, connecting all managerial levels and computing centers within the company, and be connectable to other companies' platforms.

3. The project must generate hard-dollar savings through productivity gains that are quantifiable in advance, and it should be rolled out in stages to ensure that it is delivering those hard-dollar savings.

4. The project must be managed as much as an *organizational* initiative as a technology initiative. Installing a powerful electronic platform without redesigning how work is performed and how decisions are made will not tap its true potential.

Installing InterAAct is partly a matter of faith. But $150 million projects cannot be justified on faith alone. After extensive study (including in-depth analyses of how 300 AMR employees from different parts of the company actually spend their time), we estimated that extensive automation could produce enough hard-dollar savings to generate a 10% return on the InterAAct investment. AMR's standard hurdle rate is 15%, so corporate directors with a pure financial mind-set would not have approved this project. That's where faith comes in. We are confident that the "soft-dollar" benefits—better decisions, faster procedures, more effective customer service—will boost returns on InterAAct well above the hurdle rate. Still we are rolling out the project in stages and testing its impact along the way to be sure the hard-dollar savings materialize first.

I don't know how InterAAct will change our company's organizational structure and work practices

> Down the road, a company appointing a new CIO will seem as odd as a company today naming a vice president for water and gas.

over the next five years. But I guarantee there will be major changes. Most large companies are organized to reflect how information flows inside them. As electronic technologies create new possibilities for extending and sharing access to information, they make possible new kinds of organizations. Big companies will enjoy the benefits of scale without the burdens of bureaucracy. Information technology will drive the transition from corporate hierarchies to networks. Companies will become collections of experts who form teams to solve specific business problems and then disband. Information technology will blur distinctions between centralization and decentralization; senior managers will be able to contribute expertise without exercising authority.[4]

We are currently at work on a series of InterAAct applications to reduce common sources of frustration and delay within AMR. Why should employees remain in the dark about the status of resource requests? On-line forms and electronic signature control, to be introduced later this year, will help speed such approval processes. Why should an employee's personnel file remain locked away and inaccessible? A pilot project at the Dallas/Fort Worth airport allows baggage handlers to use a workstation to check how much overtime they have accrued. Eventually, employees should be able to file their own insurance claims or check on their reimbursement status. With respect to bureaucratic procedures, the potential of an electronic platform is obvious: eliminate paper, slash layers, speed decisions, simplify the information flows.

---

4. For a good overview of the organizational possibilities, see Lynda M. Applegate, James I. Cash, Jr., and D. Quinn Mills, "Information Technology and Tomorrow's Manager," HBR November-December 1988, p. 128.

Other organizational possibilities are even more far-reaching. InterAAct standardizes spreadsheets and databases, provides direct access to the corporate mainframes, and will eventually support automatic report generation. The new ease and speed with which analysts will be able to accumulate and disaggregate data, conduct "what if" scenarios, and share information should accelerate the planning and budgeting process. It's not our job to design a new planning process. InterAAct gives our analysts the potential to redesign systems to best suit their needs.

Finally, and perhaps of greatest importance, InterAAct will allow senior executives to make their presence felt more deeply without requiring more day-to-day control. Eventually, executives should be able to practice selective intervention. The information system, by virtue of its comprehensiveness, will alert senior managers to pockets of excellence or trouble and allow them to take appropriate action more quickly. Over time, the role of management will change from overseeing and control to resolving important problems and transferring best practices throughout the organization.

Who Needs the CIO?

The ultimate impact of the hardware, software, and organizational developments I have described is to proliferate and decentralize technology throughout the organization. Piece by piece and brick by brick, we and others are building a corporate information infrastructure that will touch every job and change relationships between jobs. Much work remains to be done. We need better tools, more connectivity, and richer data that reflect the real business needs of our companies. But in all these areas, momentum is moving in the right direction.

As technology reshapes the nature of work and redefines organizational structures, technology itself will recede into the strategic background. Eventually—and we are far from this time—information systems will be thought of more like electricity or the telephone network than as a decisive source of organizational advantage. In this world, a company trumpeting the appointment of a new chief information officer will seem as anachronistic as a company today naming a new vice president for water and gas. People like me will have succeeded when we have worked ourselves out of our jobs. Only then will our organizations be capable of embracing the true promise of information technology.

Reprint 90307

Managers can release the real power of computers by challenging centuries-old notions about work.

Reengineering Work: Don't Automate, Obliterate

by Michael Hammer

Despite a decade or more of restructuring and downsizing, many U.S. companies are still unprepared to operate in the 1990s. In a time of rapidly changing technologies and ever-shorter product life cycles, product development often proceeds at a glacial pace. In an age of the customer, order fulfillment has high error rates and customer inquiries go unanswered for weeks. In a period when asset utilization is critical, inventory levels exceed many months of demand.

The usual methods for boosting performance— process rationalization and automation—haven't

Use computers to redesign— not just automate— existing business processes.

yielded the dramatic improvements companies need. In particular, heavy investments in information technology have delivered disappointing results—largely because companies tend to use technology to mechanize old ways of doing business. They leave the existing processes intact and use computers simply to speed them up.

But speeding up those processes cannot address their fundamental performance deficiencies. Many of our job designs, work flows, control mechanisms, and organizational structures came of age in a different competitive environment and before the advent of the computer. They are geared toward efficiency and control. Yet the watchwords of the new decade are innovation and speed, service and quality.

It is time to stop paving the cow paths. Instead of embedding outdated processes in silicon and software, we should obliterate them and start over. We should "reengineer" our businesses: use the power of modern information technology to radically redesign our business processes in order to achieve dramatic improvements in their performance.

Every company operates according to a great many unarticulated rules. "Credit decisions are made by the credit department." "Local inventory is needed for good customer service." "Forms must be filled in completely and in order." Reengineering strives to break away from the old rules about how we organize

Michael Hammer is president of Hammer and Company, an information technology consulting firm in Cambridge, Massachusetts. This article is based in part on work performed in association with the Index Group, also a Cambridge-based consultancy.

and conduct business. It involves recognizing and rejecting some of them and then finding imaginative new ways to accomplish work. From our redesigned processes, new rules will emerge that fit the times. Only then can we hope to achieve quantum leaps in performance.

Reengineering cannot be planned meticulously and accomplished in small and cautious steps. It's an all-or-nothing proposition with an uncertain result. Still, most companies have no choice but to muster the courage to do it. For many, reengineering is the only hope for breaking away from the antiquated processes that threaten to drag them down. Fortunately, managers are not without help. Enough businesses have successfully reengineered their processes to provide some rules of thumb for others.

What Ford and MBL Did

Japanese competitors and young entrepreneurial ventures prove every day that drastically better levels of process performance are possible. They develop products twice as fast, utilize assets eight times more productively, respond to customers ten times faster. Some large, established companies also show what can be done. Businesses like Ford Motor Company and Mutual Benefit Life Insurance have reengineered their processes and achieved competitive leadership as a result. Ford has reengineered its accounts payable processes, and Mutual Benefit Life, its processing of applications for insurance.

In the early 1980s, when the American automotive industry was in a depression, Ford's top management put accounts payable – along with many other departments – under the microscope in search of ways to cut costs. Accounts payable in North America alone employed more than 500 people. Management thought that by rationalizing processes and installing new computer systems, it could reduce the head count by some 20%.

Ford was enthusiastic about its plan to tighten accounts payable – until it looked at Mazda. While Ford was aspiring to a 400-person department, Mazda's accounts payable organization consisted of a total of 5 people. The difference in absolute numbers was astounding, and even after adjusting for Mazda's smaller size, Ford figured that its accounts payable organization was five times the size it should be. The Ford team knew better than to attribute the discrepancy to calisthenics, company songs, or low interest rates.

Ford managers ratcheted up their goal: accounts payable would perform with not just a hundred but many hundreds fewer clerks. It then set out to achieve it. First, managers analyzed the existing system. When Ford's purchasing department wrote a purchase order, it sent a copy to accounts payable. Later, when material control received the goods, it sent a copy of the receiving document to accounts payable. Meanwhile, the vendor sent an invoice to accounts payable. It was up to accounts payable, then, to match the purchase order against the receiving document and the invoice. If they matched, the department issued payment.

The department spent most of its time on mismatches, instances where the purchase order, receiving document, and invoice disagreed. In these cases, an accounts payable clerk would investigate the discrepancy, hold up payment, generate documents, and all in all gum up the works.

One way to improve things might have been to help the accounts payable clerk investigate more efficiently, but a better choice was to prevent the mismatches in the first place. To this end, Ford instituted "invoiceless processing." Now when the purchasing department initiates an order, it enters the information into an on-line database. It doesn't send a copy of the purchase order to anyone. When the goods arrive at the receiving dock, the receiving clerk checks the database to see if they correspond to an outstanding purchase order. If so, he or she accepts them and enters the transaction into the computer system. (If receiving can't find a database entry for the received goods, it simply returns the order.)

Under the old procedures, the accounting department had to match 14 data items between the re-

Why did Ford need 400 accounts payable clerks when Mazda had just 5?

ceipt record, the purchase order, and the invoice before it could issue payment to the vendor. The new approach requires matching only three items – part number, unit of measure, and supplier code – between the purchase order and the receipt record. The matching is done automatically, and the computer prepares the check, which accounts payable sends to the vendor. There are no invoices to worry about since Ford has asked its vendors not to send them. (See the diagram, "Ford's Accounts Payable Process...," for illustrations of the old and new payables processes.)

Ford didn't settle for the modest increases it first envisioned. It opted for radical change – and achieved dramatic improvement. Where it has instituted this new process, Ford has achieved a 75% reduction in head count, not the 20% it would have gotten with a conventional program. And since there are no discrepancies between the financial record and the physical record, material control is simpler and financial information is more accurate.

Mutual Benefit Life, the country's eighteenth largest life carrier, has reengineered its processing of insurance applications. Prior to this, MBL handled customers' applications much as its competitors did. The long, multistep process involved credit checking, quoting, rating, underwriting, and so on. An application would have to go through as many as 30 discrete steps, spanning 5 departments and involving 19 people. At the very best, MBL could process an application in 24 hours, but more typical turnarounds ranged from 5 to 25 days – most of the time spent passing information from one department to the next. (Another insurer estimated that while an application spent 22 days in process, it was actually worked on for just 17 minutes.)

MBL's rigid, sequential process led to many complications. For instance, when a customer wanted to cash in an existing policy and purchase a new one, the old business department first had to authorize the treasury department to issue a check made payable to MBL. The check would then accompany the paperwork to the new business department.

The president of MBL, intent on improving customer service, decided that this nonsense had to stop and demanded a 60% improvement in productivity. It was clear that such an ambitious goal would require more than tinkering with the existing process. Strong measures were in order, and the management team assigned to the task looked to technology as a means of achieving them. The team realized that shared databases and computer networks could make many different kinds of information available to a single person, while expert systems could help people with limited experience make sound decisions. Applying these insights led to a new approach to the application-handling process, one with wide organizational implications and little resemblance to the old way of doing business.

MBL swept away existing job definitions and departmental boundaries and created a new position called a case manager. Case managers have total responsibility for an application from the time it is received to the time a policy is issued. Unlike clerks, who performed a fixed task repeatedly under the watchful gaze of a supervisor, case managers work autonomously. No more handoffs of files and responsibility, no more shuffling of customer inquiries.

Case managers are able to perform all the tasks associated with an insurance application because they are supported by powerful PC-based workstations that run an expert system and connect to a range of automated systems on a mainframe. In particularly tough cases, the case manager calls for assistance from a senior underwriter or physician, but these spe-

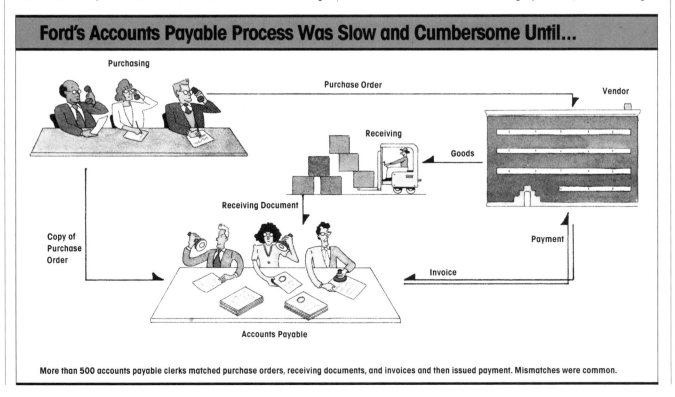

Ford's Accounts Payable Process Was Slow and Cumbersome Until...

More than 500 accounts payable clerks matched purchase orders, receiving documents, and invoices and then issued payment. Mismatches were common.

cialists work only as consultants and advisers to the case manager, who never relinquishes control.

Empowering individuals to process entire applications has had a tremendous impact on operations. MBL can now complete an application in as little as four hours, and average turnaround takes only two to five days. The company has eliminated 100 field office positions, and case managers can handle more than twice the volume of new applications the company previously could process.

The Essence of Reengineering

At the heart of reengineering is the notion of discontinuous thinking—of recognizing and breaking away from the outdated rules and fundamental assumptions that underlie operations. Unless we change these rules, we are merely rearranging the deck chairs on the Titanic. We cannot achieve breakthroughs in performance by cutting fat or automating existing processes. Rather, we must challenge old assumptions and shed the old rules that made the business underperform in the first place.

Every business is replete with implicit rules left over from earlier decades. "Customers don't repair their own equipment." "Local warehouses are necessary for good service." "Merchandising decisions are made at headquarters." These rules of work design are based on assumptions about technology, people, and organizational goals that no longer hold. The contemporary repertoire of available information technologies is vast and quickly expanding. Quality, innovation, and service are now more important than cost, growth, and control. A large portion of the population is educated and capable of assuming responsibility, and workers cherish their autonomy and expect to have a say in how the business is run.

It should come as no surprise that our business processes and structures are outmoded and obsolete: our work structures and processes have not kept pace with the changes in technology, demographics, and business objectives. For the most part, we have organized work as a sequence of separate tasks and employed complex mechanisms to track its progress. This arrangement can be traced to the Industrial Revolution, when specialization of labor and economies of scale promised to overcome the inefficiencies of cottage industries. Businesses disaggregated work into narrowly defined tasks, reaggregated the people performing those tasks into departments, and installed managers to administer them.

Our elaborate systems for imposing control and discipline on those who actually do the work stem from the postwar period. In that halcyon period of expansion, the main concern was growing fast without going broke, so businesses focused on cost, growth, and control. And since literate, entry-level people were abundant but well-educated professionals hard

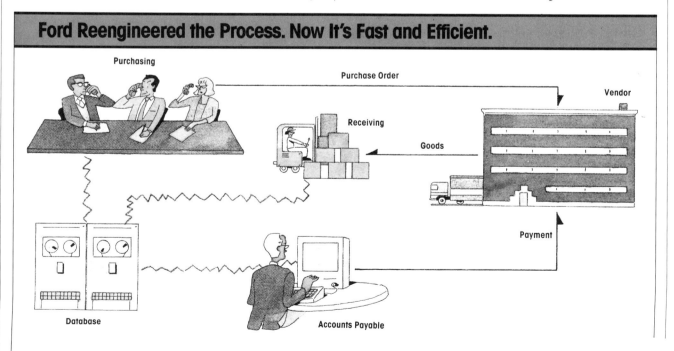

Ford Reengineered the Process. Now It's Fast and Efficient.

The new process cuts head count in accounts payable by 75%, eliminates invoices, and improves accuracy. Matching is computerized.

to come by, the control systems funneled information up the hierarchy to the few who presumably knew what to do with it.

These patterns of organizing work have become so ingrained that, despite their serious drawbacks, it's hard to conceive of work being accomplished any other way. Conventional process structures are fragmented and piecemeal, and they lack the integration necessary to maintain quality and service. They are breeding grounds for tunnel vision, as people tend to substitute the narrow goals of their particular

> **Ford's old rule: we pay when we get the invoice.**
> **Ford's new rule: we pay when we get the goods.**

department for the larger goals of the process as a whole. When work is handed off from person to person and unit to unit, delays and errors are inevitable. Accountability blurs, and critical issues fall between the cracks. Moreover, no one sees enough of the big picture to be able to respond quickly to new situations. Managers desperately try, like all the king's horses and all the king's men, to piece together the fragmented pieces of business processes.

Managers have tried to adapt their processes to new circumstances, but usually in ways that just create more problems. If, say, customer service is poor, they create a mechanism to deliver service but overlay it on the existing organization. Bureaucracy thickens, costs rise, and enterprising competitors gain market share.

In reengineering, managers break loose from outmoded business processes and the design principles underlying them and create new ones. Ford had operated under the old rule that "We pay when we receive the invoice." While no one had ever articulated or recorded it, that rule determined how the accounts payable process was organized. Ford's reengineering effort challenged and ultimately replaced the rule with a new one: "We pay when we receive the *goods*."

Reengineering requires looking at the fundamental processes of the business from a cross-functional perspective. Ford discovered that reengineering only the accounts payable department was futile. The appropriate focus of the effort was what might be called the goods acquisition process, which included purchasing and receiving as well as accounts payable.

One way to ensure that reengineering has a cross-functional perspective is to assemble a team that represents the functional units involved in the process being reengineered and all the units that depend on it. The team must analyze and scrutinize the existing process until it really understands what the process is trying to accomplish. The point is not to learn what happens to form 73B in its peregrinations through the company but to understand the purpose of having form 73B in the first place. Rather than looking for opportunities to improve the current process, the team should determine which of its steps really add value and search for new ways to achieve the result.

The reengineering team must keep asking Why? and What if? Why do we need to get a manager's signature on a requisition? Is it a control mechanism or a decision point? What if the manager reviews only requisitions above $500? What if he or she doesn't see them at all? Raising and resolving heretical questions can separate what is fundamental to the process from what is superficial. The regional offices of an East Coast insurance company had long produced a series of reports that they regularly sent to the home office. No one in the field realized that these reports were simply filed and never used. The process outlasted the circumstances that had created the need for it. The reengineering study team should push to discover situations like this.

In short, a reengineering effort strives for dramatic levels of improvement. It must break away from conventional wisdom and the constraints of organizational boundaries and should be broad and cross-functional in scope. It should use information technology not to automate an existing process but to enable a new one.

Principles of Reengineering

Creating new rules tailored to the modern environment ultimately requires a new conceptualization of the business process—which comes down to someone having a great idea. But reengineering need not be haphazard. In fact, some of the principles that companies have already discovered while reengineering their business processes can help jump start the effort for others.

Organize around outcomes, not tasks. This principle says to have one person perform all the steps in a process. Design that person's job around an objective or outcome instead of a single task. The redesign at Mutual Benefit Life, where individual case managers perform the entire application approval process, is the quintessential example of this.

The redesign of an electronics company is another example. It had separate organizations performing each of the five steps between selling and installing the equipment. One group determined customer requirements, another translated those requirements into internal product codes, a third conveyed that information to various plants and warehouses, a fourth received and assembled the components, and a fifth delivered and installed the equipment. The process was based on the centuries-old notion of specialized labor and on the limitations inherent in paper files. The departments each possessed a specific set of skills, and only one department at a time could do its work.

The customer order moved systematically from step to step. But this sequential processing caused problems. The people getting the information from the customer in step one had to get all the data anyone would need throughout the process, even if it wasn't needed until step five. In addition, the many handoffs were responsible for numerous errors and misunderstandings. Finally, any questions about customer requirements that arose late in the process had to be referred back to the people doing step one, resulting in delay and rework.

When the company reengineered, it eliminated the assembly-line approach. It compressed responsibility for the various steps and assigned it to one person, the "customer service representative." That person now oversees the whole process—taking the order, translating it into product codes, getting the components assembled, and seeing the product delivered and installed. The customer service rep expedites and coordinates the process, much like a general contractor. And the customer has just one contact, who always knows the status of the order.

Have those who use the output of the process perform the process. In an effort to capitalize on the benefits of specialization and scale, many organizations established specialized departments to handle specialized processes. Each department does only one type of work and is a "customer" of other groups' processes. Accounting does only accounting. If it needs new pencils, it goes to the purchasing department, the group specially equipped with the information and expertise to perform that role. Purchasing finds vendors, negotiates price, places the order, inspects the goods, and pays the invoice—and eventually the accountants get their pencils. The process works (after a fashion), but it's slow and bureaucratic.

Now that computer-based data and expertise are more readily available, departments, units, and individuals can do more for themselves. Opportunities exist to reengineer processes so that the individuals who need the result of a process can do it themselves. For example, by using expert systems and databases, departments can make their own purchases without sacrificing the benefits of specialized purchasers. One manufacturer has reengineered its purchasing process along just these lines. The company's old system, whereby the operating departments submitted requisitions and let purchasing do the rest, worked well for controlling expensive and important items like raw materials and capital equipment. But for inexpensive and nonstrategic purchases, which constituted some 35% of total orders, the system was slow and cumbersome; it was not uncommon for the cost of the purchasing process to exceed the cost of the goods being purchased.

The new process compresses the purchase of sundry items and pushes it on to the customers of the process. Using a database of approved vendors, an operating unit can directly place an order with a vendor and charge it on a bank credit card. At the end of the month, the bank gives the manufacturer a tape of all credit card transactions, which the company runs against its internal accounting system.

When an electronics equipment manufacturer reengineered its field service process, it pushed some

> Must technicians make repairs? Or can computers help customers make their own?

of the steps of the process on to its customers. The manufacturer's field service had been plagued by the usual problems: technicians were often unable to do a particular repair because the right part wasn't on the van, response to customer calls was slow, and spare-parts inventory was excessive.

Now customers make simple repairs themselves. Spare parts are stored at each customer's site and managed through a computerized inventory-management system. When a problem arises, the customer calls the manufacturer's field-service hot line and describes the symptoms to a diagnostician, who accesses a diagnosis support system. If the problem appears to be something the customer can fix, the diagnostician tells the customer what part to replace and how to install it. The old part is picked up and a new part left in its place at a later time. Only for complex problems is a service technician dispatched to the site, this time without having to make a stop at the warehouse to pick up parts.

When the people closest to the process perform it, there is little need for the overhead associated managing it. Interfaces and liaisons can be nated, as can the mechanisms used to coor those who perform the process with those wh

> ## Why Did We Design Inefficient Processes?
>
> In a way, we didn't. Many of our procedures were not designed at all; they just happened. The company founder one day recognized that he didn't have time to handle a chore, so he delegated it to Smith. Smith improvised. Time passed, the business grew, and Smith hired his entire clan to help him cope with the work volume. They all improvised. Each day brought new challenges and special cases, and the staff adjusted its work accordingly. The hodgepodge of special cases and quick fixes was passed from one generation of workers to the next.
>
> We have institutionalized the ad hoc and enshrined the temporary. Why do we send foreign accounts to the corner desk? Because 20 years ago, Mary spoke French and Mary had the corner desk. Today Mary is long gone, and we no longer do business in France, but we still send foreign accounts to the corner desk. Why does an electronics company spend $10 million a year to manage a field inventory worth $20 million? Once upon a time, the inventory was worth $200 million, and managing it cost $5 million. Since then, warehousing costs have escalated, components have become less expensive, and better forecasting techniques have minimized units in inventory. But the inventory procedures, alas, are the same as always.
>
> Of the business processes that *were* designed, most took their present forms in the 1950s. The goal then was to check overambitious growth — much as the typewriter keyboard was designed to slow typists who would otherwise jam the keys. It is no accident that organizations stifle innovation and creativity. That's what they were *designed* to do.
>
> Nearly all of our processes originated before the advent of modern computer and communications technology. They are replete with mechanisms designed to compensate for "information poverty." Although we are now information affluent, we still use those mechanisms, which are now deeply embedded in automated systems.

Moreover, the problem of capacity planning for the process performers is greatly reduced.

Subsume information-processing work into the real work that produces the information. The previous two principles say to compress linear processes. This principle suggests moving work from one person or department to another. Why doesn't an organization that produces information also process it? In the past, people didn't have the time or weren't trusted to do both. Most companies established units to do nothing but collect and process information that other departments created. This arrangement reflects the old rule about specialized labor and the belief that people at lower organizational levels are incapable of acting on information they generate. An accounts payable department collects information from purchasing and receiving and reconciles it with data that the vendor provides. Quality assurance gathers and analyzes information it gets from production.

Ford's redesigned accounts payable process embodies the new rule. With the new system, receiving, which produces the information about the goods received, processes this information instead of sending it to accounts payable. The new computer system can easily compare the delivery with the order and trigger the appropriate action.

Treat geographically dispersed resources as though they were centralized. The conflict between centralization and decentralization is a classic one. Decentralizing a resource (whether people, equipment, or inventory) gives better service to those who use it, but at the cost of redundancy, bureaucracy, and missed economies of scale. Companies no longer have to make such trade-offs. They can use databases, telecommunications networks, and standardized processing systems to get the benefits of scale and coordination while maintaining the benefits of flexibility and service.

At Hewlett-Packard, for instance, each of the more than 50 manufacturing units had its own separate purchasing department. While this arrangement provided excellent responsiveness and service to the plants, it prevented H-P from realizing the benefits of its scale, particularly with regard to quantity discounts. H-P's solution is to maintain the divisional purchasing organizations and to introduce a corporate unit to coordinate them. Each purchasing unit has access to a shared database on vendors and their performance and issues its own purchase orders. Corporate purchasing maintains this database and uses it to negotiate contracts for the corporation and to monitor the units. The payoffs have come in a 150% improvement in on-time deliveries, 50% reduction in lead times, 75% reduction in failure rates, and a significantly lower cost of goods purchased.

Link parallel activities instead of integrating their results. H-P's decentralized purchasing operations represent one kind of parallel processing in which separate units perform the same function. Another common kind of parallel processing is when separate units perform different activities that must eventually come together. Product development typically operates this way. In the development of a photocopier, for example, independent units develop the various subsystems of the copier. One group works on the optics, another on the mechanical paper-handling device, another on the power supply, and so on. Having people do development work simultaneously saves time, but at the dreaded integration and testing phase, the pieces often fail to work together. Then the costly redesign begins.

Or consider a bank that sells different kinds of credit—loans, letters of credit, asset-based financing—through separate units. These groups may have no way of knowing whether another group has already

> Coordinate parallel functions *during* the process—not after it's completed.

extended credit to a particular customer. Each unit could extend the full $10 million credit limit.

The new principle says to forge links between parallel functions and to coordinate them while their activities are in process rather than after they are completed. Communications networks, shared databases, and teleconferencing can bring the independent groups together so that coordination is ongoing. One large electronics company has cut its product development cycle by more than 50% by implementing this principle.

Put the decision point where the work is performed, and build control into the process. In most organizations, those who do the work are distinguished from those who monitor the work and make decisions about it. The tacit assumption is that the people actually doing the work have neither the time nor the inclination to monitor and control it and that they lack the knowledge and scope to make decisions about it. The entire hierarchical management structure is built on this assumption. Accountants, auditors, and supervisors check, record, and monitor work. Managers handle any exceptions.

The new principle suggests that the people who do the work should make the decisions and that the process itself can have built-in controls. Pyramidal management layers can therefore be compressed and the organization flattened.

Information technology can capture and process data, and expert systems can to some extent supply knowledge, enabling people to make their own decisions. As the doers become self-managing and self-controlling, hierarchy—and the slowness and bureaucracy associated with it—disappears.

When Mutual Benefit Life reengineered the insurance application process, it not only compressed the linear sequence but also eliminated the need for lay-

GEOMETRIC DUDS

GOOFBALL

BLOCKHEAD

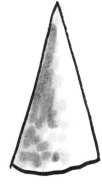

DUNCE

CLOD

ers of managers. These two kinds of compression—vertical and horizontal—often go together; the very fact that a worker sees only one piece of the process calls for a manager with a broader vision. The case managers at MBL provide end-to-end management of the process, reducing the need for traditional managers. The managerial role is changing from one of controller and supervisor to one of supporter and facilitator.

Capture information once and at the source. This last rule is simple. When information was difficult to transmit, it made sense to collect information repeatedly. Each person, department, or unit had its own requirements and forms. Companies simply had to live with the associated delays, entry errors, and costly overhead. But why do we have to live with those problems now? Today when we collect a piece of information, we can store it in an on-line database for all who need it. Bar coding, relational databases, and electronic data interchange (EDI) make it easy to collect, store, and transmit information. One insurance company found that its application review process required that certain items be entered into "stovepipe" computer systems supporting different functions as many as five times. By integrating and connecting these systems, the company was able to eliminate this redundant data entry along with the attendant checking functions and inevitable errors.

Think Big

Reengineering triggers changes of many kinds, not just of the business process itself. Job designs, organizational structures, management systems—anything associated with the process—must be refashioned in an integrated way. In other words, reengineering is a tremendous effort that mandates change in many areas of the organization.

When Ford reengineered its payables, receiving clerks on the dock had to learn to use computer terminals to check shipments, and they had to make decisions about whether to accept the goods. Purchasing agents also had to assume new responsibilities—like making sure the purchase orders they entered into the database had the correct information about where to send the check. Attitudes toward vendors also had to change: vendors could no longer be seen as adversaries; they had to become partners in a shared business process. Vendors too had to adjust. In many cases, invoices formed the basis of their accounting systems. At least one Ford supplier adapted by continuing to print invoices, but instead of sending them to Ford threw them away, reconciling cash received against invoices never sent.

The changes at Mutual Benefit Life were also widespread. The company's job-rating scheme could not accommodate the case manager position, which had a lot of responsibility but no direct reports. MBL had to devise new job-rating schemes and compensation policies. It also had to develop a culture in which people doing work are perceived as more important than those supervising work. Career paths, recruitment and training programs, promotion policies—these and many other management systems are being revised to support the new process design.

The extent of these changes suggests one factor that is necessary for reengineering to succeed: executive leadership with real vision. No one in an organization wants reengineering. It is confusing and disruptive and affects everything people have grown accustomed to. Only if top-level managers back the effort and outlast the company cynics will people take reengineering seriously. As one wag at an electronics equipment manufacturer has commented, "Every few months, our senior managers find a new religion. One time it was quality, another it was customer service, another it was flattening the organization. We just hold our breath until they get over it and things get back to normal." Commitment, consistency—maybe even a touch of fanaticism—are needed to enlist those who would prefer the status quo.

Considering the inertia of old processes and structures, the strain of implementing a reengineering plan can hardly be overestimated. But by the same token, it is hard to overestimate the opportunities, especially for established companies. Big, traditional organizations aren't necessarily dinosaurs doomed to extinction, but they are burdened with layers of unproductive overhead and armies of unproductive workers. Shedding them a layer at a time will not be good enough to stand up against sleek startups or streamlined Japanese companies. U.S. companies need fast change and dramatic improvements.

We have the tools to do what we need to do. Information technology offers many options for reorganizing work. But our imaginations must guide our decisions about technology—not the other way around. We must have the boldness to imagine taking 78 days out of an 80-day turnaround time, cutting 75% of overhead, and eliminating 80% of errors. These are not unrealistic goals. If managers have the vision, reengineering will provide a way.

Reprint 90406

Target information for competitive performance

Robert E. Cole

A simple system is sometimes best, as Japanese practices show

Corporate managers have largely ignored the potential of their information systems for shaping strategy. Now that the electronic revolution makes available to companies extraordinary amounts and kinds of information, as fast as they want it, executives need to examine their practices more closely. By comparing the information-gathering systems of U.S. companies with those of Japan, this author shows that the way companies use information shapes policy, intentionally or not. He also points out the importance of getting information to those who need it, and says that the complex, computerized system is not always the most effective for improving competitive performance.

Mr. Cole is professor of sociology and research associate for the Center for Japanese Studies at the University of Michigan. He is currently in Washington, D.C. as a Woodrow Wilson Center fellow and is working on a book on participatory work practices in the United States, Sweden, and Japan. His last book was Work, Mobility, and Participation: A Comparative Study of American and Japanese Industry *(University of California Press, 1979).*

Illustrations by Richard A. Goldberg.

As everyone knows, the information age is upon us. The electronic revolution makes available to companies data unprecedented in scale and accessibility. The media emphasize the new technology's potential for providing decision-making information in forms previously nonexistent. Computerized systems, for example, can release information simultaneously throughout an organization as events are taking place, thereby extending top management's control. The new systems can monitor processes and people and integrate their actions to a greater extent than ever before. They permit in-depth financial modeling and analysis of alternative scenarios. The implications of the new technology for shaping strategy and increasing predictability are reported to be enormous.

Yet many discussions focus on the new technology's intrinsic characteristics and how they affect the shape, scope, and depth of information and pay little attention to how this revolution affects organizational performance. The boosters of the new technology sometimes fail to consider the impediments to effective decision making that complex information systems can erect when their output creates information overload and finely honed models that are far removed from reality. Simpler information systems are often more efficient for carrying out simpler tasks.

Preliminary evidence suggests that we should question the conventional wisdom concerning computers and productivity. Paul Strassman's pilot study of 40 firms, using 200 measurements from each firm concludes that there is no direct and simple correlation between managerial productivity and information technology.[1]

Author's note: Support from the Joint U.S.-Japan Automotive Study provided the initial opportunity to pursue this subject. Among my colleagues who were helpful with ideas and data, I would particularly like to thank Michael Flynn, John Campbell, Vladimir Pucik, and Gerald Ross. I alone am responsible for the conclusions drawn from these contributions.

Editor's note: All references the end of the article.

In this article I look at information systems as a factor in economic performance. My research on inventory control systems, participatory work practices, quality assurance, problem solving, and reward systems has uncovered some common patterns in the treatment of information. My objective is not to show that clever manipulation of information systems is the key to successful economic performance but to demonstrate that a company's approach to information systems affects other strategies in a way that significantly affects economic performance. Thus I stress a systemic approach to improved economic performance rather than any single magic key.

Uses of information

To gain a full understanding of its significance for business performance, information must be seen broadly. Using a dictionary definition of information as knowledge gained through communication, I will ask the following questions in the course of this article: What is the extent of choice and selectivity available in information systems (are systems neutral)? What are the determinants of the information we collect (when do we measure)? What kinds of bias distorts in the information being transmitted? Indeed, how do we decide what constitutes information? How does the monitoring of information systems balance off organizational control with problem solving?

Other issues include: how information systems provide managers with assurance that they are good managers; how information systems serve the interests of those with power in the organization; what the difference is between communication and involvement with regard to information flow; how information systems inhibit or facilitate organizational change; finally, how information systems relate to technology and in particular to the role of the computer.

Underlying these issues is a set of tensions between the need to use information for control (for accounting systems, for example) and the need to extend to individuals at all organizational levels information of such an amount and quality that they can contribute as much as possible to formulating and achieving organizational objectives.

Why is information important? At the most elementary level, when we collect certain information on a regular basis, we focus attention on it. By collecting and aggregating it, we convey the impression it is at least somewhat important. This in turn enhances the possibility that a demand will arise for the use of it. Conversely, information we don't collect may be seen as unimportant. Until recently, few U.S. companies in the consumer goods industries, for example, conducted comprehensive quality audits. This lack both reflected and contributed to quality being seen as a less significant organizational goal.

Biased information

My view of information runs counter to a perspective that sees information and accounting systems as neutral in their impacts on organizational behavior. According to a neutral perspective, information systems are resources that can aid decision makers in many ways; how they are used determines their impact. Some information systems offer less discretion to decision makers than others, however, and therefore they lead to organizational rigidity. Other kinds of information systems lead organizations to anticipate problems better and to experiment and innovate; that is, they foster organizational flexibility. Still another reason information and accounting systems are seldom neutral is that information is subject to strategic misrepresentation. Since information is commonly used by someone to persuade someone else of something, it is subject to a certain amount of distortion.

Consider the emphasis in Japanese companies on eliciting and implementing employee suggestions. In the mid-1970s employee suggestions at Toyota were running about 385,000 a year, or roughly about 8.5 a person. In 1981 the company received 1,412,500 suggestions — an average of more than 31 suggestions per employee. Moreover, Toyota reported a significant rise in the number of suggestions adopted over this period, with the implementation rate rising to an amazing 94% in 1981.

It is clear to close observers that there has been a tremendous inflation of results in response to top management pressure. Workers feel great pressure to submit suggestions and often they will make quite trivial proposals just to get management off their backs. Similarly, companies inflate the acceptance rate through various practices, including not counting the proposals in calculating the implementation rate until they have passed an initial screening.

In a survey of quality circle activity with 100 respondents from various Japanese companies, Shoji Shiba found that 20% reported such practices as fabricating ghost QC meetings, inflating results of QC activities, and making up fake stories about quality circles. Such "window dressing," as Shiba calls it, appears rampant in response to the pressure at each level to produce results.[2] Similarly, workers know that their job evaluations will reflect the success of their QC activities. These realities often lead to collusion.

High-level managers are not necessarily unaware of such practices. They may tolerate them in order to build an aura of success around the movement for individual employee contributions to the company. Nor are such practices unknown in the United States. In one auto plant I studied, a foreman reported that, under strong pressure from his boss to increase the number of employee suggestions, he started writing them himself and getting friendly workers to sign them.

One might assume that a primary objective of information systems in modern business organizations is to contribute to greater efficiency in achieving organizational goals. Yet it is important to understand that, historically, accounting systems, the major determinants of information flow in business organizations, reflected the separation of management from ownership. Accountancy thus assumed a custodial role, and its objective was more to keep tabs on assets than to contribute to organizational efficiency as such.

Accountancy systems have gradually changed and become more concerned with efficiency. In fact, the basis of today's accounting model aims "to get more with less"; this is a powerful tool within the parameters of the model. Yet the ability of the accounting model to change is limited by its fundamental principles: it is a closed system model, it balances perfectly and in this sense is totally mechanistic, and it exerts enormous pressures for standardization through measurement demands.

The problem in applying such systems to maximize organizational efficiency is that organizations operate in open systems with uncertain environments—they are organic rather than mechanistic because the whole is sometimes greater than the sum of its parts. Pressures for standardization often stifle initiative and discourage risk.

Two final introductory points are in order. First, organizations tend to collect information that meets the needs of those with power in the organization. The cliché that knowledge is power does have some truth to it. Second, most organizations gather more information than they use, which suggests a problem of linking information to decisions. Despite the glut, organizational decision makers constantly complain that they still don't have enough information. I will pursue this theme later.

Japanese systems

Continuing comparisons of American and Japanese manufacturing companies show that overall the Japanese operate with more selective and often simpler information systems. This observation has significant organizational implications. To be sure, in some areas the Japanese do collect more systematic information, such as in mapping their external environment. In particular, they appear to gather more comprehensive data with regard to consumer preference and on the international competitive environment. Leonard Lynn, for example, shows how Japan's rise to a position of world leadership in the steel industry is linked with its effective surveillance of international developments in technology.[3] As is typical with such a scanning function, the Japanese collected more information than they needed.

With respect to internal operations, however, particularly in control of the manufacturing process, the Japanese appear to operate with more selective information systems than do the Americans. Our study at the University of Michigan of the auto industry found that the finance and accounting departments, two main generators of the demand for information, accounted for 8% to 10% of total salaried employees in the U.S. companies but for only 2% in one of the major Japanese auto manufacturers. This does not mean that Japanese companies don't operate with strict financial controls. Rather, they delegate this function to line managers (especially with their related-group companies), who are close to the action. Use of dual controls, with all the implications for duplication of paperwork and staff time, is infrequent.

Having more selective and often simpler information systems for controlling the manufacturing process, the Japanese concentrate their data collection to provide information for continuous improvement in quality and productivity. When they learn about the system of documentation necessary for adopting Japanese quality systems, American executives are often struck by how extensive it is. The Japanese focus less on measuring the costs of quality, however, than on information geared to upgrading quality. Moreover, officials at the Japanese Union of Scientists and Engineers point out that the large data demands that concern the Americans are transitory; once the necessary information brings the manufacturing process under control, data demands sharply decline.

Kanban

Consider the just-in-time delivery system, or kanban, practiced by suppliers and original equipment manufacturers (OEMs) in Japan. Versions of this system are spreading rapidly to U.S. manufacturers. As is well known by now, the just-in-time method greatly shortens the production lead time from entry of materials to product completion because all processes in the production chain produce the necessary parts at the necessary time with only the minimum stock on hand. For American manufacturers accustomed to storing large stocks of in-process inventory, this requires a drastic change. But the savings associated with these inventory reductions have inspired many U.S. companies.

American manufacturers commonly use quite elaborate and expensive inventory control systems that depend on complicated computer routines. Materials requirement planning, for example, uses procedures that require extensive paperwork, materials bills, lead-time estimates, inventory, records, and master production schedules. As a consequence, MRP depends on computers.

Unfortunately, the history of elegant inventory control systems in the United States is that they don't last very long. International Data Systems estimates that approximately $10 billion has been spent thus far on MRP systems but that only 25% of these systems has achieved installation objectives. I wonder how long even these will be successful.

We can think about the just-in-time delivery system as an information network that serves important signaling functions. The term *kanban* refers literally to a block of wood that tells the supplier, or the person who represents the immediate upstream process, to refill a particular order. Instead of a complicated master plan, each link in the production chain simply draws the parts it needs to complete its schedules from the preceding link. (Americans use this system in restocking supermarkets.) Zenzaburo Katayama, assistant manager of Toyota's Total Quality Control Promotion Department, captures the system's essential elements:

"Although we use computers for working out monthly production schedules and production volumes, our daily variations of production are all controlled by the movement of kanban. If we were to use computers for the fine tuning of the production schedules in lieu of kanban, we would probably need a capacity 20 times what we now have. Moreover, even with such computing capabilities we would not be able to do all the jobs that kanban does for us. No computer program can predict the fluctuations in automobile production. A central feature of the Toyota production system is the way information is processed and utilized. Where the computer falls short, we use other means such as kanban and cards attached to the body of each automobile. We expect our workers to use their brains to read and interpret such information and signals from the kanban, cards, etc., and we also expect them to contribute toward refining the system by providing new ideas."[4]

Several points stand out from these observations. First, a simple information system relies on direct information flows located close to the relevant decision makers. As a consequence, the system allows for immediate feedback from those most concerned (the production workers) and thereby permits rapid corrective action. The system is effective not only in handling in-process inventory efficiently but also in reducing waste, uncovering bottlenecks, improving quality, minimizing plant space, and allowing for rapid change in product lines. Computer-based data processing systems, by contrast, are often slow (in an organizational sense), complex, and management centered. The Japanese have adopted computer and other advanced technology, but I am struck in going through their manufacturing plants by how selective their processes are and how often they give quality as the reason for automating a particular process.

I am not suggesting that kanban has no problems. Small suppliers have complained that they sometimes have to bear the costs of goods they produced that customers cancelled at the last minute. Indeed, this matter was serious enough to become the subject of Japanese Diet deliberations just a few years ago. Moreover, the reduction of in-process inventories allows no buffers that permit workers more control over their work pace. Buffer strategies have been central to many efforts to increase participatory work practices as a remedy to mechanistic work measurement (Taylorization), especially in Sweden.

In our sample of 245 suppliers of raw materials, parts, and components to the OEMs in the auto industry, more than 70% reported some implementation of just-in-time systems by early 1984. The lower than usual level of inventory building during the U.S. economy's recovery stage in early 1984 suggests that just-in-time delivery systems are taking hold in many manufacturing companies. Reports suggest that this change is driven mainly by the immediate payoffs from reduced costs of holding inventory and the availability of new technology (for example, electronic cash registers).

Companies are paying less attention to the implications of such systems for interorganizational relationships. Auto suppliers in our survey, for example, reported little progress in reducing the volatility of orders even though such information exchanges become all the more critical with the reduced production lead time that just-in-time delivery systems allow. The implications of such systems for production and quality functions are not yet fully known.

As is the case with all aspects of organizational design, there is no best way to handle information. The design must always depend on the tasks to be performed and other conditions of the organization's environment. For some tasks, complete control of vast quantities of information and the interrelationships among variables is necessary for maintaining operations. Consider the task of sending a rocket to the moon. Not only must one computer simultaneously control an incredible number of variables in a situation

where failure of a minor component can lead to a catastrophe, but two or three computers must also be running simultaneously to provide backup if one fails.

A supermarket does not need such elaborate controls. The manager just wants to be sure the shelves are stocked, to be aware of what is selling well and what is selling poorly, to be able to track the high-cost items, and to develop systems for handling financial concerns. Some supermarket chains do develop more elaborate systems, but the marginal returns on these are low.

The point I am trying to make here is that Japanese producers have been inclined to treat the tasks required for making an automobile more like operating a supermarket than launching a rocket, while the American attitude, until recently, was the other way around. More important perhaps than making this generalization is to point out the tremendous stress the Japanese place on finding ways to simplify the manufacturing process. The just-in-time system is a good example of this.

U.S. systems

The discussion so far suggests the need for some rethinking. Information systems usually have as their chief purposes the monitoring of performance in the whole range of a company's critical operations so as to help control its direction. *Monitor* is the key term, and it can mean a number of things. On the one hand, the word reflects the fact that accounting systems are basically tools of mistrust. We monitor to ensure that everyone is playing according to Hoyle and that each unit is performing as it's supposed to. We provide information in the form of standard operating procedure to deal with recurrent problems. This is as true in Japan as it is in the United States.

But monitoring has other implications as well. We monitor our operations so that we can identify emerging problems and have the information to solve them. This function is critical to organizational survival. It means that we have to collect information and make it available in ways that ensure that our organizations will be flexible, resilient, and capable of responding to rapid changes in the environment.

This problem-identification and problem-solving function often gets lost in American corporations. Many U.S. companies have overly elaborate measurement systems that are in effect powerful control mechanisms for distributing punishments and rewards. As William Ouchi said: "Those insisting upon clear and precise measurement for the purpose of advancing individual interests must have an elaborate information system."⁵ Under such conditions, the problem-identification and problem-solving function becomes trivialized. Risk taking is discouraged.

The financial management system's requirements are often so detailed that they don't allow managers the flexibility for trading off resources. Failure to meet a single line-item objective often causes management to overreact and overcontrol. Hasty corrective action further distorts objectives. To be effective, managers need to be able to blend resources to achieve desired outcomes. Heavy stress, for example on reducing head counts, can lead them to ignore creative uses of their manpower. Situations of overcontrol also arise because top executives fundamentally distrust employees at all levels. In the basic manufacturing industries, this mistrust reflects in part traditional adversarial relations between management and labor as well as the different ethnic, racial, and religious backgrounds of workers and management. An economic system in which rapid turnover and job transfers are the norm can also create lack of trust.

Under such conditions, U.S. managers rely on complex information systems to socialize employees to appropriate organizational behavior and to serve as a basis for evaluating performance. Formal records and instructions are the underpinnings of such a system. In addition, many companies have top-heavy staffs and highly differentiated layering and sectionalism in their middle management. U.S. companies that have tried to move toward the just-in-time delivery system report great difficulty in getting finance managers to agree to a shift in responsibility for monitoring work-in-process costs from finance to manufacturing departments. This is a classic example of the conflict between the control and the problem-solving functions of information systems.

In our auto study, we found that although some companies were successful in their efforts to reduce the number of layers in their plant hierarchies, plant managers were still six or seven layers away from chief executives. Japanese plant managers are at most two layers away, and they often serve on company boards of directors. All these layers in U.S. companies and the associated perquisites and corporate staffs seem to call for an increased flow of information to inform everyone and control everything. The kinds of information systems we have and the way we evaluate our management personnel appear to be related. For example, in the auto study, the Japanese companies relied more than U.S. companies do on employee opinions concerning the success of past training efforts and future training objectives; that is, they relied more on upward information flows.

In summary, Japanese companies generally have fewer management levels, a more homogeneous labor force, and lower employee turnover. Their management appraisals rely less on top-down informa-

tion. Thus their monitoring systems operate less as tools of distrust and providers of criteria for distributing rewards and punishments. Instead their information systems identify problems, perform preventive maintenance, and provide the raw material for problem solving.

This process operates in participative management practices. As is now well known, quality circles, the small, blue-collar problem-solving groups that proliferated in the early 1960s and are now spreading rapidly to service sector firms, are a key element in Japanese participative management strategy. Quality circles have spread rapidly throughout the United States in recent years. Japanese companies have no elaborate systems for measuring such factors as quality circles' return on investment. Rather, the circles themselves report to management on the projects they are working on, and if management chooses a solution a circle suggests, the circle often provides estimates of the expected savings. Then it is easy to calculate the number of circle projects, the rate of suggestion implementation, and estimated savings. This simple system keeps the circles' emphasis on problem solving.

When American managers first visited Japanese factories to study quality circles, they often asked managers there how they knew whether the circles were really contributing to the bottom line, what their ROI was, and so forth. The usual Japanese reaction was "Let's go out on the shop floor and I will show you." There they pointed to improvements on this and that machine or in a procedure and said, "See, this is what Yamashita-san did," or "This is what Suzuki-san did." The Japanese were, in short, willing to rely on their line managers' reports that the circles were really working. But the Americans kept coming and asking the same questions, and the Japanese managers, not liking to be embarrassed, started creating the numbers that the Americans were requesting such as percentage of productivity increase accounted for by a circle.

Some Japanese companies even produced slick publications to publicize this information. Now the Americans go home and say, "See, they do it the same way we do." So much for increased cross-cultural communication.

Quality circles

Many U.S. companies measure quality circle results through existing and newly added management information systems. In our survey of 176 early adopters of quality circles in the United States, 36% reported using existing measurement systems to evaluate quality circle performance, 5% had developed new measurement systems, 25.5% were using a combination, and 33.5% had no measurement system. The last group reported a notably lower level of success. American companies clearly have a strong need to show bottom-line results. It's as if to be good managers we must collect information. Gathering facts seems to provide a ritualistic assurance of appropriate decision making and thus of good management.

Japanese managers may well be subject to these same pressures. Indeed, their quality improvement effort's ideology strongly stresses the need to make decisions based on facts, not experience. But Japanese managers, as we have seen, are much more likely to accept employee-gathered data as legitimate.

The collection of information as a tool of suspicion also applies to quality circles. At a major U.S. aerospace company the person in charge of the quality circle program told me that one day, on two hours' notice, he had to make a presentation to his division manager showing the circles' effectiveness. He understood that if he was not convincing, management would discontinue the program. This occurred after the company had invested more than a year in developing and implementing the program. The program manager said to me, "This is management by terrorism."

To understand this situation better, one may ask, when do we measure? One answer is that we measure, as in the case just described, when innovations threaten our basic values. Then, the measurement systems are often designed to show that proposals won't work. When a situation involves technological innovation, management feels much less constrained to measure (Herbert Simon noted this when he analyzed American managers' decisions to buy computers). When social innovations threaten basic values concerning the distribution of power, authority, and competence, however, managers—especially U.S. middle managers—often demand careful measurements and bottom-line results. Quality circles threaten many middle management prerogatives (who can, and has the right to, solve problems?) and represent a way of running a business that alarms many managers. Our early adopter survey data consistently show that resistance from middle managers is seen as the biggest obstacle to quality circle success.

Japanese middle managers also resisted quality circles at first, and they had to be educated to change. Japanese executives are more inclined, however, to assume that they will be more successful if they mobilize all the company's human resources, so they find quality circles less threatening. This explains why the Japanese placed less emphasis on measuring the circles' contribution and why they were willing to rely on circle members' reports. High-level management decisions supported the initiation of circle activities; this was followed by the collection and selective distribution of case study data results to spread the message. Japanese management used measurement to publicize the innovation, not to question its utility. The Swedes take a similar approach to participative management.

Information sharing

What do companies need from information systems to better operate their businesses? Companies are best served by systems that are simple, that can deliver information to those who need it for doing their day-to-day jobs, and that deliver information in a usable form. Let's look at these three requirements. A common problem management faces at all levels is information overload. The Texas Instruments slogan, "More than two objectives is no objective," may be exaggerated, but it makes the point well. Too much information leads to a lack of clarity in priorities. Furthermore, too much information in the form of guidelines for action leads to reduced employee discretion and therefore a loss of employee initiative.

Second, a good system delivers information to those who need it for doing their day-to-day work. American corporations collect a lot of information, but management doesn't always put it in the hands of those who need it. Consider the quality audits that I discussed earlier. A number of companies are now conducting such audits and making comprehensive assessments of the costs of poor quality. This, of course, is not an end in itself; rather, the objective is to put the results of these studies in the hands of operating people so that they can take corrective action. Unfortunately, in a number of corporations top management is using these audits to reward and punish its division heads rather than making them available to operating personnel. In his comparative study of product quality in the Japanese and U.S. air conditioner industry, David Garvin concluded the same thing. He stated, "The Japanese firms consistently pushed quality data down to the lowest possible level of the organization, in order to educate the work force, while the American companies normally aggregated upwards, in order to provide middle and upper management with useful summaries."[6]

Getting information into the hands of the people who need it has predictable effects. At one U.S. plant I visited, the plant manager proudly told me in the morning that his policy was to answer union grievances in three words or less. He was showing me how tough he was. But later that day, he complained that the union made his life difficult by coming up with the most outrageous demands. He didn't seem to make a connection between his two statements. He didn't see that if you give people little or no information they can construct "outrageous" interpretations of what is happening.

Finally, it is not enough to get information to the people who need it. It must be in a usable form, particularly for problem identification and problem solving. Three kinds of information typically available in a manufacturing plant include: production data, scrap data, and warranty data. But is this information available to people on the shop floor in a simple and usable form? Grouped production data are commonly available, but production data by machine are seldom available to the shop floor. If this information is available by machine, the workers can begin to start thinking about uptime and machine maintenance. Scrap data are also commonly obtainable, but how often are they disaggregated in ways that have meaning to the average shop floor worker? Only if these data can be related to the particular job is the worker likely to show any interest.

Information sharing is clearly a major feature of Japanese organizational practices and is closely related to other methods for which they have become noted. Japanese quality assurance methods, for example, are characterized by high levels of information sharing with all employees, which encourages employees to take significant responsibility for improving quality. Information sharing underlies Japanese participatory work practices, provides a basis for trust, and serves as a resource for identifying and solving problems. Toyota, for example, revitalized its quality circles in the 1970s by funneling customer warranty data to production workers. In general, the Japanese share information with production workers that American companies often don't make available even to second-level supervisors.

For information sharing to create a basis of trust between employees and managers, it must not only be targeted and relevant to individual workers' jobs but also be presented in a nonevaluative manner. General Motors discovered not long ago that sharing information such as financial data to compare plants creates competition among work forces and can lead to resentment among workers as well as unions.

At Volvo, however, a recent evaluation concluded that heightening competition over high quality and low costs among separate assembly operations had positive outcomes. This contradictory result suggests the need for more research into the aims of information sharing and the conditions for success. Success in sharing information is more likely when trust and a high-quality labor force already exist. Persisting adversarial relationships, especially in our mature manufacturing industries, reduce the basis for trust and therefore the benefits information sharing can produce.

Similarly, the poor quality of the American labor force as measured by the high level of functional illiteracy and poor mathematical skills, relative to our Japanese competitors, means we can obtain less from information sharing than we might hope for. Increasingly, information is quantitatively expressed. Information sharing is a good strategy for developing trust and improving the quality of labor, but it is a slow process.

U.S. companies that adopt participatory work practices, such as small problem-solving groups, without making sincere efforts to increase information flow to workers face tough sledding. If management wants small problem-solving groups and self-managing work teams to take more responsibility for operations, it must develop accounting information relevant to their needs. Such information has been slow to develop.

Employee feedback

A general principle of the participatory movement is to put decision making where the information is, in order to reflect the fact that ordinary workers have a lot more information in their heads than management usually recognizes. While it is true that workers often have information they don't share with management, it is also true that management has a lot of information it doesn't share with employees. So the slogan "put the information where the decision ought to be" also makes sense. Indeed, a critical objective ought to be supplying feedback information throughout the organization, as it relates to the achievement of specific organizational goals.

So far, I have stressed moving information down through the organization by a strategy of information sharing. Clearly, it is also important to move information up. In research on comparative quality levels, I found that the Japanese emphasis on achieving better and continuous manufacturing feedback to engineering was a major element in their success in improving quality. Information about what is happening on the shop floor leads to continuous design modification, and blue collar workers are an essential part of that process.

Yet many U.S. manufacturing plants cover up information rather than share it. In a survey of 80 U.S. operating nuclear power plants, the Nuclear Regulatory Commission reported 6½ times more emergency shutdowns in U.S. facilities than in similarly designed Japanese plants. The report attributed this in part to the Americans' reluctance to share information, so that corrective action was often short lived or inadequate. Despite many common problems, facilities did not share information sufficiently. Generally speaking, I have found that a great deal of the failure to share information results – to return to an earlier theme – from fears among workers in U.S. facilities that management would use the information primarily to punish or reward people rather than for solving problems.

A new study of the well-known Kalmar plant built by Volvo in 1974, which was conducted in 1984 by work organization experts from Swedish national unions and the employers' federation, reported outstanding progress in quality standards, cost reduction, and inventory turnover. The Kalmar initiative was earlier written off by American observers, who criticized the plant on the grounds that, despite its advanced participatory work practices, it was not suitable for high-volume production. The Swedish researchers concluded that the information-sharing strategy was critical to the success of the Kalmar management efforts.

Specifically, after a strategy that involved pushing information from the top down, the Kalmar plant changed to a more successful system of using information to directly involve employees with the specific economic problems affecting their workshop. The company achieved this involvement through a variety of mechanisms including delegating the budget-making process deeper into the organization.

Also, management kept the unions closely informed about the budget-making process and the unions helped pass on information. They also had an opportunity to register their views. This is in striking contrast to the way U.S. companies decide what information employees need to carry out their daily activities. The scope can be far broader than American management's customary emphasis on PR and simple communication. Beating employees over the head with information on the loss of American markets and jobs to foreign companies simply won't get us very far.

Underlying American attitudes toward information is a corresponding attitude toward planning. In many U.S. companies, managers believe they know the best way to put a complex product together before they are actually working with the people and the machines. Another possible planning approach uses a more iterative process that draws on interaction during the implementation of machines and processes. The latter method takes into account changing environmental conditions, which implies that no one most effective approach exists. Rather, a continuous adaptive process is necessary. Implicit is a view of the planning process as only the beginning of the learning process, that we operate in a world of imperfect information in which implementation teaches us how to maximize effective performance. Put differently, this view of planning sees people and machines as defined by their roles; thus, performance can be maximized only in the course of implementation.

The first, typically American, model involves a mechanical view of people and machines:

Recommended readings

The U.S. and Japanese Automobile Industries in Transition: Report of the Joint U.S.-Japan Automotive Study, ed. Robert E. Cole and Taizo Yakushiji (Ann Arbor: University of Michigan, Center for Japanese Studies, 1984).

Bo Hedberg and Sten Jonsson, "Designing Semi-Confusing Information Systems for Organizations in Changing Environments," Accounting, Organizations and Society, vol. 3 (Oxford: Pergamon Press, 1978).

Anders Malmberg, "The Impact of Job Reform on Accounting Systems," Managing and Developing New Forms of Work Organization, Management Development Series No. 16 (Geneva: International Labour Office, 1981).

Martha Feldman and James March, "Information in Organizations as Signal and Symbol," Administrative Science Quarterly 26 (1981), 171.

"They are what they are." Such thinking implies that one can incorporate in the planning process most of what is necessary to maximize organizational performance before putting any people or machines on the shop floor or in the office. These two models are extreme characterizations of the planning process. Real situations are complex, with shadings and tendencies toward one method or the other. The General Motors Saturn project for designing a small car, which is unprecedented in a number of respects, illustrates this complexity well. It broke new ground at GM by bringing large numbers of people together, including workers and union leaders, to devise the "best product and process designs in the world, making maximum use of human resources." I don't mean to detract from the company's achievement by what I say about the project.

GM organized seven technical groups along traditional lines (for example, engine group and chassis group) and set up seven parallel study teams to develop the work organization, with a total of 99 employees (65 United Auto Workers and 34 General Motors people). The communication between the parallel technical and nontechnical groups, to the extent that it existed, assumed for the most part that the technical demands would set the parameters for organizing the work.

The employees didn't know the exact nature of the product they were planning, where it would be built (greenfield versus established plant), or how autonomous the new car's organization would be, which made it difficult for the study teams to make their efforts practical. Trying to plan technical and nontechnical systems separately, then put them together mechanically, does not allow for the kind of continuous learning process the second planning model suggests. In the Saturn project, the matter was further complicated by the uncertainty of subsequent job assignments for those associated with the planning process. Thus the opportunities created for continuous learning were significantly limited.

The planning for the Saturn project is at least two steps removed from the reality of the learning that must take place to effectively organize a project. First, the technical and nontechnical system planning must take place together and, second, management must arrange the process so that everyone involved sees it as a continuing, interactive process. These two conditions are normal operating procedure in large Scandinavian manufacturing plants because their managements more or less accept the sociotechnical model. In Scandinavian companies, however, union involvement is typically far less than it was in the GM Saturn project.

In this article, I have compared Japanese and American practices to highlight the role and uses of information in business. Participative work practices, quality assurance issues, and inventory systems serve to clarify alternative strategies and the interaction of information systems with these strategies. Although U.S. companies know about and have used in varying degrees the strategies discussed here, most companies do not use systematically information systems to improve organizational performance.

References

1 Paul Strassman, Information Payoff: The Transformation of Work in an Electronic Age (New York: Free Press, 1985).

2 Shoji Shiba, "Concealed Creeping Disease Called 'Window-Dressing' Widely Prevalent," Japan Economic Journal, June 28, 1983, p. 31.

3 Leonard Lynn, How Japan Innovates: A Comparison with the United States in the Case of Oxygen Steelmaking (Boulder, Colo.: Westview Press, 1982).

4 Zenzaburo Katayama, "What One Must Do Before Applying [sic] Kanban System," lecture supplements from a three-day seminar on kanban, quality control, and quality management (Tokyo: Cambridge Corporation, 1983).

5 William Ouchi, Theory Z: How American Business Can Meet the Japanese Challenge (Reading, Mass.: Addison-Wesley, 1981).

6 David A. Garvin, "Japanese Quality Management," Columbia Journal of World Business, Fall 1984, p. 3.

Reprint 85305

HBR CASE STUDY

Why should Middleton fund an IS project with "intangible" benefits? But what if it doesn't?

The Case of the Soft Software Proposal

by Thomas H. Davenport

Middleton Mutual is a large insurance company headquartered in Philadelphia. Its chief information officer, Dennis Devereaux, and vice president of information systems planning, Max Vargo, are about to request $1 million to develop an expert system for Linda Peterson's property and casualty (P&C) underwriting department. They've discussed the expert system with President Bill Hayes, CFO Hal Atkins, and other members of the capital expense committee and until now have felt confident it would be approved. But according to the messages in the company's electronic mailbox, the project seems less certain.

**Welcome to Middleton E-mail.
You have 1 new message.**

To: **DDevereaux, CIO**
From: **MVargo, VP, IS planning**
 Finished the paperwork for expert systems underwriting program. Expected benefits are soft – intangibles like more consistent underwriting and faster turnaround – but compelling. Absent any big changes, we can get it to Capital Expense Committee for next week's meeting. Are you checking with Bill Hayes? I'll check if you want.

**Welcome to Middleton E-mail.
You have 1 new message.**

To: **WHayes, president**
From: **DDevereaux, CIO**
 Just wanted to confirm that we will be submitting our expert systems proposal to the CEC next week. We've pinned down the figures, and they're well within the $1 million we budgeted. We've selected a shell program from a first-rate vendor and lined up a top-notch knowledge engineering consultant who specializes in insurance applications. Two of our most experienced underwriters and eight programmers from my department will work closely with the consultant. We're excited about this program and are anxious to get started.

**Welcome to Middleton E-mail.
You have 1 new message.**

To: **DDevereaux, CIO**
From: **WHayes, president**
 Sorry I haven't had a chance to get to you sooner. Given last quarter's results, we're not in a position to approve any projects that don't pay for themselves almost immediately. Be sure your justification form shows concrete and immediate financial benefits. Promises of "better service" won't cut it.

**Welcome to Middleton E-mail.
You have 1 new message.**

To: **WHayes, president**
From: **DDevereaux, CIO**
 Bill, this isn't like replacing 50 people with a computer in the back office. How can you quantify staying in business? I thought we agreed this was the first step to get Middleton on a level IS playing field. You remember the progression: first, the expert system for multiperil, then we take it to commercial auto and workers' comp. Next we'll upgrade the mainframes and connect our databases and other systems with the expert systems. When we're all connected, we'll be ready for our ultimate goal of letting agents analyze risk and quote policies on the spot. If we delay, we'll be left in the dust. I've seen it in other companies – you try to save a few dollars, and you wind up broke.

**Welcome to Middleton E-mail.
You have 1 new message.**

To: **DDevereaux, CIO**
From: **WHayes, president**
 I'd like to see you do the project, but we need to know what the payoff is. Everything should have a number attached. If expert systems are more efficient, the committee will want to know how much more efficient. I'm just cautioning you to be straightforward about the financial implications.

Thomas H. Davenport is senior research associate at the Harvard Business School.

**Welcome to Middleton E-mail.
You have 1 new message.**

To: **HAtkins, CFO**
From: **WHayes, president**
Any more thoughts on the expert systems project? Dennis may not be able to document concrete savings, but I keep looking over my shoulder at companies that are getting into this artificial intelligence business — Cigna, Travelers, USAA, Fireman's Fund. I heard about an expert system that analyzed an application and said to write it at substandard when the company's best underwriter had decided it was standard. They reexamined the case and found out the underwriter was wrong.

**Welcome to Middleton E-mail.
You have 1 new message.**

To: **WHayes, president**
From: **HAtkins, CFO**
I think we should stand firm on this unless we see convincing numbers. It looks to me like another black hole we'll keep throwing money into. We can't afford any more runaway technology projects. Devereaux says he wants to get us into laptops, but he doesn't have any idea whether that's going to cut our administrative costs or underwriting losses or what. He's got a technology solution looking for a problem. If he can prove there are direct productivity benefits, he'll have my support. But we're getting hit from all sides — taxes, interest rates, soft prices. I'm worried about next quarter. And the quarter after that.

**Welcome to Middleton E-mail.
You have 1 new message.**

To: **LPeterson, VP, P&C**
From: **DDevereaux, CIO**
Some members of the CEC, including Bill Hayes, are leaning against the expert system project. I know I've got your support on this, but I'd appreciate it if you'd let Bill and Hal know that you're behind the project. They don't seem to realize that this application has very real benefits for your department.

**Welcome to Middleton E-mail.
You have 1 new message.**

To: **DDevereaux, CIO**
From: **LPeterson, VP, P&C**
Sorry to hear the committee is going against your proposal, but I don't think I can say anything to change the outcome. Bill and Hal are running things by the numbers. Roger Lerch, my best underwriter, is retiring in six months, and Lucy Townsend and Henry Ballard are going next year. That kind of experience is hard to replace. But let's not worry too much about it. I can get something started under my budget — which is how things usually work around here. If I didn't use the back door, I'd have an abacus on my desk. Besides, my people will accept it better if we take the lead. Right now, the underwriters say there's too much judgment involved for expert systems to do their job. They have to get used to the idea.

**Welcome to Middleton E-mail.
You have 1 new message.**

To: **LPeterson, VP, P&C**
From: **DDevereaux, CIO**
I haven't given up on the project, and I've budgeted for it. It's just a matter of convincing Hal and Bill that it's worth the money. A word from you would certainly reinforce the idea that there's a real business need.

**Welcome to Middleton E-mail.
You have 1 new message.**

To: **MVargo, VP, IS planning**
From: **DDevereaux, CIO**
This is going to be a harder sell than I thought. I'm sure Hal Atkins has talked Bill out of it. Atkins is dead set against technology investments of any kind unless they have immediate financial benefits. Why don't you put together some fancy slides of the data you got — show how expert systems make fewer mistakes than human experts and how much time it takes to process an application with and without the system. Use some of the material the vendors gave us. And reserve the conference room for Monday afternoon. Meanwhile, I'll decide how to play this — shelve the proposal for now or give Bill and Hal the numbers they want, even if they're half-baked.

**Welcome to Middleton E-mail.
You have 1 new message.**

To: **DDevereaux, CIO**
From: **MVargo, VP, IS planning**
Not surprised Atkins is giving this department a hard time. Maybe we should do development in-house. We can promise less trouble with integration and more functionality with a customized system. DP can do the project. We can hire a knowledge engineer to work with programmers who are interested in artificial intelligence rule sets and neural networks — things other companies are afraid of. Should I talk to the guys in DP?

**Welcome to Middleton E-mail.
You have 1 new message.**

To: **MVargo, VP, IS planning**
From: **DDevereaux, CIO**
Let's not reopen the make-buy issue. I'm firm on using a shell. If we produce a functional stand-alone system in months instead of years, we won't get our water turned off. Then we can tackle the integration. Just get the data and sit on this for now. Don't discuss it with anyone in DP, and whatever you do, don't talk about neural networks or neural-computing with anyone outside the department. People might get the wrong idea about what we're trying to do.

**Welcome to Middleton E-mail.
You have 1 new message.**

To: **JParker, secretary**
From: **LPeterson, VP, P&C**
Joan, let me know how much is left in our budget for office supplies and furniture. Also, get me a list of our approved software vendors. And set up a meeting with Roger Lerch and Lucy Townsend. I have a special project for them.

What Do the Experts Say about the Expert System?

Three IS executives and one systems consultant analyze Middleton's situation.

Hayes must decide for himself if the project is important.

All the ingredients for a major debacle are present at Middleton. The expert systems proposal is intended to make a fundamental change in the way the company does business, but it is being presented and judged as an information technology project.

Only the line organizations can justify investing in the expert systems proposal by projecting improvements in their operating performance, and they do not appear to be partners in the proposal. If Atkins accepts Devereaux's "half baked" numbers and approves the project, it is unlikely the returns will be achieved and very unlikely they will be measurable because the line groups that must use the tools and deliver the payoff will have no ownership or commitment.

If, on the other hand, Atkins thinks he can control investment in information technology tools by not funding this project, he is in for a surprise. The likely scenario is that each underwriting group will undertake a separate covert project to introduce expert systems. Each will be on a different schedule and will use a different vendor. The multiple development efforts and learning-curve

IRMA WYMAN *is vice president of corporate information management for Honeywell, Inc. in Minneapolis, Minnesota.*

experiences will mean wasted time and money. Integrating the various expert systems into existing databases and other systems will be problematic, and agents will face chaos rather than a single interface when they are trying to give customers quotes.

Apparently, senior management has a track record of not leading in the application of information technology. Peterson implies that bootlegging expenditures that have been formally rejected is a way of life at Middleton. Bill Hayes must take the leadership role. He needs to decide for himself whether expert systems are needed to keep his business competitive. The answer to that question will come from his line units, not from the information technology people. If he believes that this project is required for the organization's survival, then he must formalize the vision and sell it to the company as a whole.

A fascination with information technology tools must not be allowed to overshadow issues of whether the tools can and will be used and how their product will affect the business. No matter how impressive the technology, it will not produce good returns unless the people who must interact with it want to make it work. Peterson is right: the project will not be successful unless the underwriters take the lead. And fancy slides from Vargo showing that underwriters make more mistakes than expert systems is not likely to get them on his side!

If Hayes decides to go ahead with this proposal, he should let the line organizations take the lead while he stays focused on the companywide framework into which each unit's work will fit. Peterson, clearly ready to have a go at this, should be funded to develop a prototype from which business returns can be predicted. Devereaux's group should be accountable for the broader framework and should have a clearly assigned role in the prototype effort. The project's objectives should be set jointly, so Peterson and Devereaux win or lose together. Meanwhile, Hayes and Atkins must be alert to underground projects that are inconsistent with the overall framework.

The ultimate goal of agents being able to quote policies "on the spot" should be highlighted and communicated throughout the organization. Otherwise, the impression that this is a ploy to put underwriters out of a job will demotivate precisely those people who are key to the project's success.

Find the users who need the technology — and sell, sell, sell.

THOMAS L. PETTIBONE *is vice president, information systems, for New York Life Insurance Company.*

Today's CIO faces a dilemma. Well-structured computer systems are crucial to a company's long-term competitiveness. But users want their needs met fast, which often means "quick and dirty" solutions that are the antithesis of the company's long-term architectural strategy. To cope, the CIO must be both visionary and implementer.

He (or she) must envision the company's technological architecture three to five years hence and understand in a general way what building blocks must be in place to get there. He must then develop a marketing plan to get users to embrace the necessary technologies. But a CIO won't be in office for long if he pursues architecture at the expense of his users' near-term business requirements. He must also keep users content, even when their needs deviate from the envisioned architecture.

The best way to proceed is to identify needs and wants in the user community that the new technologies can satisfy. (It is always easier to appeal to those who have a need than to try to force it on those who don't.) If the vision of the future is accurate, the technologies will be of help somewhere in the organization. Then the CIO must sell, sell, sell. If he can persuade profit-center heads that the technologies will help them accomplish their objectives, they will carry the banner and sell the technology to others. The CIO must also sell senior management on the need to clean up the quick and dirty solutions to bring them in line with the long-range architectural plan.

Dennis Devereaux is smart to recognize the need for artificial intelligence. This is a technology the company cannot afford to ignore. But he is not a businessman. Devereaux has not developed a constituency of peers to help "pull" AI technology into the culture. He is trying to ramrod the technology on its own merits rather than getting users to embrace it. He should have worked with Peterson, who is his real customer, sooner. She has the business need that can help Devereaux pull AI in.

Devereaux has low credibility with senior management. Apparently, he has tried to ramrod projects like this before. His desire to prepare a presentation with "half baked" numbers in the face of sure rejection underscores his credibility problem. He confronts Hayes in an almost hostile way and doesn't acknowledge the company's financial difficulty, which is the most pressing problem. Clearly, the technology issue has jumped in front of the business requirements.

Devereaux also exhibits poor leadership qualities. Vargo is aware of the political problems this project involves. Rather than taking a prudent course, Devereaux forges ahead, risking everything. His subordinates must be dismayed.

It's not too late for Devereaux. He should align forces with Peterson and help her bootleg a small version of the project. That way, he can provide technical details that are consistent with his long-term architectural goals. He should stop trying to sell the president and the CFO on "intangibles" and let a small-scale project produce some hard benefits.

Don't let IS hide behind "intangible" benefits.

JOHN D. LOEWENBERG *is senior vice president, corporate information systems, at Aetna Life & Casualty in Hartford, Connecticut.*

The dialogue in the electronic mail messages lacks one fundamental element: a clear understanding of the organization's business strategy and overall direction. Almost all IS initiatives should support the organization's business strategies and plans. Without knowing the company's direction, IS executives have a difficult time identifying and aligning with the business's most important needs.

Middleton's IS organization seems to have a technology solution looking for a problem. While the solution may have had benefits in other environments, the benefits have not been quantified here.

Past IS projects could often be justified through direct people replacements. This is not the case today. As a result, the IS community sometimes hides behind benefits that are "soft" and "intangible." IS managers need to become better at building partnerships with their users and looking at the business from the user's point of view. In the process, they will discover that they can in fact quantify many of the seemingly soft and intangible benefits.

No one at Middleton has taken the initiative to understand underwriting's business needs and to quantify the potential revenue increases and savings. The ability to underwrite faster, with fewer errors and more consistent application of underwriting rules, can lead to faster delivery to agents. Agents may become more loyal and place more business with the company – which in turn increases revenues. Also, the ability to underwrite faster means the company might get business it would otherwise have missed, which also boosts revenues. The expert system can ensure that the company's policy rates reflect the true risks. That improves profitability.

Expert systems can have a tremendous impact on how the organization is positioned for the future. They can spread the underwriting knowledge of one or two experts to the entire organization and perform some 80% of the underwriting activity automatically. Especially if the labor base compresses—as it is expected to—in the 1990s and underwriting departments are short staffed, expert systems will be important for ensuring that the company consistently follows its own underwriting rules.

Hal Atkins is really not opposed to the idea of expert systems. He just has not yet received enough facts about how the project could affect revenue and current and future expenses. The concern about the near-term expense could be alleviated by capitalizing the project. But Middleton must know that the project makes business sense to begin with.

Use expert systems in ways others can't copy – like underwriting high-risk lines.

DIOGO TEIXEIRA *is systems consultant in the New York office of McKinsey & Company.*

The approach Middleton is taking is all too common among insurers—and many other companies—when facing a decision about investing in systems technology. It is framing the decision in terms of whether the new technology is more productive than the status quo. That seemingly straightforward approach misses an important point.

Technology itself is not a competitive advantage. It is only a tool. The purposes to which that tool is directed determine whether the insurer benefits. Improving productivity, processing applications faster, and serving customers better are all laudable goals. But competitors can easily match them, so the advantages are soon washed away.

Core technology, which includes hardware, systems software, and expert systems shells, is readily available to every insurer from the same vendors. Look how PCs penetrated the insurance industry between 1982 and 1986, or how on-line terminals arrived roughly between 1972 and 1980. While the early adopters may have felt they were gaining a competitive advantage, other companies adopted the technology too. It is impossible to isolate differences in financial performance according to when the technology was installed.

The same thing is true for expert systems shells. A decade from now, most insurers will use expert systems shells and knowledge bases to assist in making routine but relatively complex decisions. (The areas of highest applicability are underwriting commercial property and casualty, life, and disability insurance and adjusting P&C or disability claims.) But while expert systems technology will improve productivity, speed application processing, and deliver better customer service, it will not lead to a competitive advantage—because everyone will have adopted it. Devereaux seems to recognize this; he just does not want to be left in the dust.

To get Middleton ahead, Hayes should think about how the company might use technology in ways others cannot easily copy. Say your company writes commercial P&C insurance for a wide range of risks, perils, coverages, and customers. No two cases are exactly alike—precisely why you need expert systems. Why not enter a high-risk line that you cannot accurately underwrite today—but could with the aid of expert systems technology?

Environmental damage liability coverage is badly needed, for example, yet most insurers are unwilling to write it because they perceive the risk as too high. Perhaps Linda Peterson should begin writing environmental liability coverage, using an expert system to codify and encapsulate the rules. With time, Peterson could garner a large share of the market, build the knowledge base into a proprietary weapon, and feed back the experience from the business into the expert system. Competitors would have smaller market shares or less experience and would thus do a poorer job of underwriting.

This strategy would be analogous to companies that have used databases to "lock in" their market positions. State Farm, Allstate, and other direct writers of auto and home owners' insurance are so big that they can discriminate personal P&C risk much better than can an agency company. Similarly, consumer credit bureaus have amassed mammoth databases on individuals' borrowing habits, which now serve as entry barriers. With 10 or 20 years of growth, knowledge bases might become as hard to replicate as some of today's databases.

If Hayes and Peterson can find a line of insurance in which better discrimination of risk could fuel a new marketing move, they would be on their way to a real competitive advantage. They need to start now, while building the knowledge base, and they need to incorporate reliance on the knowledge base into their operating procedures.

Finding the right line of business and figuring out how to gain the initial body of knowledge without going broke is difficult and risky. But that is what business is all about. One thing is for sure: simply investing in expert systems in the hope of increasing productivity will create no competitive advantage at all.

Information-Intensive Manufacturing

Four concepts show us how the factory of 1999 must be built and managed.

The Emerging Theory of Manufacturing

by Peter F. Drucker

Japanese plants turn out two or three times more cars per worker than U.S. or European plants.

We cannot build it yet. But already we can specify the "postmodern" factory of 1999. Its essence will not be mechanical, though there will be plenty of machines. Its essence will be conceptual—the product of four principles and practices that together constitute a new approach to manufacturing.

Each of these concepts is being developed separately, by different people with different starting points and different agendas. Each concept has its own objectives and its own kinds of impact. Statistical Quality Control is changing the social organization of the factory. The new manufacturing accounting lets us make production decisions as business decisions. The "flotilla," or module, organi-zation of the manufacturing process promises to combine the advantages of standardization and flexibility. Finally, the systems approach embeds the physical process of making things, that is, manufacturing, in the economic process of business, that is, the business of creating value.

As these four concepts develop, they are transforming how we think about manufacturing and how we manage it. Most manufacturing people in the United States now know we need a new theory of

---

Peter F. Drucker is the Clarke Professor of Social Science and Management at the Claremont Graduate School in Claremont, California. His most recent book is The New Realities *(Harper & Row, 1989).*

former members of Shewhart's circle, separately developed the versions used today.

The Japanese owe their leadership in manufacturing quality largely to their embrace of Deming's precepts in the 1950s and 1960s. Juran too had great impact in Japan. But U.S. industry ignored their contributions for 40 years and is only now converting to SQC, with companies such as Ford, General Motors, and Xerox among the new disciples. Western Europe also has largely ignored the concept. More important, even SQC's most successful practitioners do not thoroughly understand what it really does. Generally, it is considered a production tool. Actually, its greatest impact is on the factory's social organization.

By now, everyone with an interest in manufacturing knows that SQC is a rigorous, scientific method of identifying the quality and productivity that can be expected from a given production process in its current form so that control of both attributes can be built into the process itself. In addition, SQC can instantly spot malfunctions and show where they occur—a worn tool, a dirty spray gun, an overheating furnace. And because it can do this with a small sample, malfunctions are reported almost immediately, allowing machine operators to correct problems in real time. Further, SQC quickly identifies the impact of any change on the performance of the entire process. (Indeed, in some applications developed by Deming's Japanese disciples, computers can simulate the effects of a proposed change in advance.) Finally, SQC identifies where, and often how, the quality and productivity of the entire process can be continuously improved. This used to be called the "Shewhart Cycle" and then the "Deming Cycle"; now it is *kaizen*, the Japanese term for continuous improvement.

But these engineering characteristics explain only a fraction of SQC's results. Above all, they do not explain the productivity gap between Japanese and U.S. factories. Even after adjusting for their far greater reliance on outside suppliers, Toyota, Honda, and Nissan turn out two or three times more cars per worker than comparable U.S. or European plants do. Building quality into the process accounts for no more than one-third of this difference. Japan's major productivity gains are the result of social changes brought about by SQC.

The Japanese employ proportionately more machine operators in direct production work than Ford or GM. In fact, the introduction of SQC almost always increases the number of machine operators. But this increase is offset many times over by the sharp drop in the number of nonoperators: inspectors, above all, but also the people who do not *do* but *fix*, like repair crews and "fire fighters" of all kinds.

manufacturing. We know that patching up old theories has not worked and that further patching will only push us further behind. Together these concepts give us the foundation for the new theory we so badly need.

The most widely publicized of these concepts, Statistical Quality Control (SQC), is actually not new at all. It rests on statistical theory formulated 70 years ago by Sir Ronald Fisher. Walter Shewhart, a Bell Laboratories physicist, designed the original version of SQC in the 1930s for the zero-defects mass production of complex telephone exchanges and telephone sets. During World War II, W. Edwards Deming and Joseph Juran, both

In U.S. factories, especially mass-production plants, such nonoperating, blue-collar employees substantially outnumber operators. In some plants, the ratio is two to one. Few of these workers are needed under SQC. Moreover, first-line supervisors also are gradually eliminated, with only a handful of trainers taking their place. In other words, not only does SQC make it possible for machine operators to be in control of their work, it makes such control almost mandatory. No one else has the hands-on knowledge needed to act effectively on the information that SQC constantly feeds back.

By aligning information with accountability, SQC resolves a heretofore irresolvable conflict. For more than a century, two basic approaches to manufacturing have prevailed, especially in the United States. One is the engineering approach pioneered by Frederick Winslow Taylor's "scientific management." The other is the "human relations" (or "human resources") approach developed before World War I by Andrew Carnegie, Julius Rosenwald of Sears Roebuck, and Hugo Münsterberg, a Harvard psychologist. The two approaches have always been considered antitheses, indeed, mutually exclusive. In SQC, they come together.

Taylor and his disciples were just as determined as Deming to build quality and productivity into the manufacturing process. Taylor asserted that his "one

> **Most U.S. quality circles of the last 20 years have failed because they lacked rigorous and reliable feedback.**

right way" guaranteed zero-defects quality; he was as vehemently opposed to inspectors as Deming is today. So was Henry Ford, who claimed that his assembly line built quality and productivity into the process (though he was otherwise untouched by Taylor's scientific management and probably did not even know about it). But without SQC's rigorous methodology, neither scientific management nor the assembly line could actually deliver built-in process control. With all their successes, both scientific management and the assembly line had to fall back on massive inspection, to fix problems rather than eliminate them.

The human-relations approach sees the knowledge and pride of line workers as the greatest resource for controlling and improving quality and productivity. It too has had important successes. But without the kind of information SQC provides, you cannot readily distinguish productive activity from busyness. It is also hard to tell whether a proposed modification will truly improve the process or simply make things look better in one corner, only to make them worse overall.

Quality circles, which were actually invented and widely used in U.S. industry during World War II, have been successful in Japan because they came in after SQC had been established. As a result, both the quality circle and management have objective information about the effects of workers' suggestions. In contrast, most U.S. quality circles of the last 20 years have failed despite great enthusiasm, especially on the part of workers. The reason? They were established without SQC, that is, without rigorous and reliable feedback.

A good many U.S. manufacturers have built quality and productivity into their manufacturing processes without SQC and yet with a minimum of inspection and fixing. Johnson & Johnson is one such example. Other companies have successfully put machine operators in control of the manufacturing process without instituting SQC. IBM long ago replaced all first-line supervisors with a handful of "managers" whose main task is to train, while Herman Miller achieves zero-defects quality and high productivity through continuous training and productivity-sharing incentives.

But these are exceptions. In the main, the United States has lacked the methodology to build quality and productivity into the manufacturing process. Similarly, we have lacked the methodology to move responsibility for the process and control of it to the machine operator, to put into practice what the mathematician Norbert Wiener called the "human use of human beings."

SQC makes it possible to attain both traditional aspirations: high quality and productivity on the one hand, work worthy of human beings on the other. By fulfilling the aims of the traditional factory, it provides the capstone for the edifice of twentieth century manufacturing that Frederick Taylor and Henry Ford designed.

Bean counters do not enjoy a good press these days. They are blamed for all the ills that afflict U.S. manufacturing. But the bean counters will have the last laugh. In the factory of 1999, manufacturing accounting will play as big a role as it ever did and probably even a bigger one. But the beans will be counted differently. The new manufacturing accounting, which might more accurately be called "manufacturing economics," differs radically from traditional cost accounting in its basic concepts. Its aim is to integrate manufacturing with business strategy.

Manufacturing cost accounting (cost accounting's rarely used full name) is the third leg of the stool – the other legs being scientific management and the assembly line – on which modern manufacturing industry rests. Without cost accounting, these two could never have become fully effective. It too is American in origin. Developed in the 1920s by General Motors, General Electric, and Western Electric (AT&T's manufacturing arm), the new cost accounting, not technology, gave GM and GE the competitive edge that made them worldwide industry leaders. Following World War II, cost accounting became a major U.S. export.

But by that time, cost accounting's limitations also were becoming apparent. Four are particularly important. First, cost accounting is based on the realities of the 1920s, when direct, blue-collar labor accounted for 80% of all manufacturing costs other than raw materials. Consequently, cost accounting equates "cost" with direct labor costs. Everything else is "miscellaneous," lumped together as overhead.

These days, however, a plant in which direct labor costs run as high as 25% is a rare exception. Even in automobiles, the most labor intensive of the major industries, direct labor costs in up-to-date plants (such as those the Japanese are building in the United States and some of the new Ford plants) are down to 18%. And 8% to 12% is fast becoming the industrial norm. One large manufacturing company with a labor-intensive process, Beckman Instruments, now considers labor costs "miscellaneous." But typically, cost accounting systems are still based on direct labor costs that are carefully, indeed minutely, accounted for. The remaining costs – and that can mean 80% to 90% – are allocated by ratios that everyone knows are purely arbitrary and totally misleading: in direct proportion to a product's labor costs, for example, or to its dollar volume.

Second, the benefits of a change in process or in method are primarily defined in terms of labor cost savings. If other savings are considered at all, it is usually on the basis of the same arbitrary allocation by which costs other than direct labor are accounted for.

Even more serious is the third limitation, one built into the traditional cost accounting system. Like a sundial, which shows the hours when the sun shines but gives no information on a cloudy day or at night, traditional cost accounting measures only the costs of producing. It ignores the costs of nonproducing, whether they result from machine downtime or from quality defects that require scrapping or reworking a product or part.

Standard cost accounting assumes that the manufacturing process turns out good products 80% of the time. But we now know that even with the best SQC, nonproducing time consumes far more than 20% of total production time. In some plants, it accounts for 50%. And nonproducing time costs as much as producing time does – in wages, heat, lighting, interest, salaries, even raw materials. Yet the traditional system measures none of this.

Finally, manufacturing cost accounting assumes the factory is an isolated entity. Cost savings in the factory are "real." The rest is "speculation" – for ex-

> Traditional cost accounting can hardly justify a product *improvement*, let alone an *innovation*.

ample, the impact of a manufacturing process change on a product's acceptance in the market or on service quality. GM's plight since the 1970s illustrates the problem with this assumption. Marketing people were unhappy with top management's decision to build all car models, from Chevrolet to Cadillac, from the same small number of bodies, frames, and engines. But the cost accounting model showed that such commonality would produce substantial labor cost savings. And so marketing's argument that GM cars would lose customer appeal as they looked more and more alike was brushed aside as speculation. In effect, traditional cost accounting can hardly justify a product *improvement*, let alone a product or process *innovation*. Automation, for instance, shows up as a cost but almost never as a benefit.

All this we have known for close to 40 years. And for 30 years, accounting scholars, government accountants, industry accountants, and accounting firms have worked hard to reform the system. They have made substantial improvements. But since the reform attempts tried to build on the traditional system, the original limitations remain.

What triggered the change to the new manufacturing accounting was the frustration of factory-automation equipment makers. The potential users, the people in the plants, badly wanted the new equipment. But top management could not be persuaded to spend the money on numerically controlled machine tools or robots that could rapidly change tools, fixtures, and molds. The benefits of automated equipment, we now know, lie primarily in the reduction of nonproducing time by improving quality (that is, getting it right the first time) and by sharply curtailing machine downtime in changing over from one model or product to another. But these gains cost accounting does not document.

Out of this frustration came Computer-Aided Manufacturing-International, or CAM-I, a cooperative effort by automation producers, multinational manufacturers, and accountants to develop a new cost accounting system. Started in 1986, CAM-I is just beginning to influence manufacturing practice. But already it has unleashed an intellectual revolution. The most exciting and innovative work in management today is found in accounting theory, with new concepts, new approaches, new methodology—even what might be called new economic philosophy—rapidly taking shape. And while there is enormous controversy over specifics, the lineaments of the new manufacturing accounting are becoming clearer every day.

As soon as CAM-I began its work, it became apparent that the traditional accounting system could not be reformed. It had to be replaced. Labor costs are clearly the wrong unit of measurement in manufacturing. But—and this is a new insight—so are all the other elements of production. The new measurement unit has to be time. The costs for a given period of time must be assumed to be fixed; there are no "variable" costs. Even material costs are more fixed than variable, since defective output uses as much material as good output does. The only thing that is both variable and controllable is how much time a given process takes. And "benefit" is whatever reduces that time. In one fell swoop, this insight eliminates the first three of cost accounting's four traditional limitations.

> In the new accounting, finished-goods inventory is a sunk cost, not an asset.

But the new cost concepts go even further by redefining what costs and benefits really are. For example, in the traditional cost accounting system, finished-goods inventory costs nothing because it does not absorb any direct labor. It is treated as an "asset." In the new manufacturing accounting, however, inventory of finished goods is a "sunk cost" (an economist's, not an accountant's, term). Stuff that sits in inventory does not earn anything. In fact, it ties down expensive money and absorbs time. As a result, its time costs are high. The new accounting measures these time costs against the benefits of finished-goods inventory (quicker customer service, for instance).

Yet manufacturing accounting still faces the challenge of eliminating the fourth limitation of traditional cost accounting: its inability to bring into the measurement of factory performance the impact of manufacturing changes on the total business—the return in the marketplace of an investment in automation, for instance, or the risk in not making an investment that would speed up production changeovers. The in-plant costs and benefits of such decisions can now be worked out with considerable accuracy. But the business consequences are indeed speculative. One can only say, "Surely, this should help us get more sales," or "If we don't do this, we risk falling behind in customer service." But how do you quantify such opinions?

Cost accounting's strength has always been that it confines itself to the measurable and thus gives objective answers. But if intangibles are brought into its equations, cost accounting will only raise more questions. How to proceed is thus hotly debated, and with good reason. Still, everyone agrees that these business impacts have to be integrated into the measurement of factory performance, that is, into manufacturing accounting. One way or another, the new accounting will force managers, both inside and outside the plant, to make manufacturing decisions as *business* decisions.

Henry Ford's epigram, "The customer can have any color as long as it's black," has entered American folklore. But few people realize what Ford meant: flexibility costs time and money, and the customer won't pay for it. Even fewer people realize that in the mid-1920s, the "new" cost accounting made it possible for GM to beat Ford by giving customers both colors and annual model changes at no additional cost.

By now, most manufacturers can do what GM learned to do roughly 70 years ago. Indeed, many go quite a bit further in combining standardization with flexibility. They can, for example, build a variety of end products from a fairly small number of standardized parts. Still, manufacturing people tend to think like Henry Ford: you can have either standardization at low cost or flexibility at high cost, but not both.

The factory of 1999, however, will be based on the premise that you not only *can* have both but also *must* have both—and at low cost. But to achieve this, the factory will have to be structured quite differently.

Today's factory is a battleship. The plant of 1999 will be a "flotilla," consisting of modules centered either around a stage in the production process or around a number of closely related operations. Though overall command and control will still exist, each module will have its own command and control. And each, like the ships in a flotilla, will be maneuverable, both in terms of its position in the entire process and its relationship to other modules. This organization will give each module the benefits of standardization and, at the same time, give the whole process greater flexibility. Thus it will allow rapid changes in design and product, rapid response to market demands, and low-cost production of "options" or "specials" in fairly small batches.

No such plant exists today. No one can yet build it. But many manufacturers, large and small, are moving toward the flotilla structure: among them are some of Westinghouse's U.S. plants, Asea Brown Boveri's robotics plant in Sweden, and several large printing plants, especially in Japan.

The biggest impetus for this development probably came from GM's failure to get a return on its massive (at least $30 billion and perhaps $40 billion) investment in automation. GM, it seems, used the new machines to improve its existing process, that is, to make the assembly line more efficient. But the process instead became less flexible and less able to accomplish rapid change.

Meanwhile, Japanese automakers and Ford were spending less and attaining more flexibility. In these plants, the line still exists, but it is discontinuous rather than tightly tied together. The new equipment is being used to speed changes, for example, automating changeovers of jigs, tools, and fixtures. So the line has acquired a good bit of the flexibility of traditional batch production without losing its standardization. Standardization and flexibility are thus no longer an either-or proposition. They are—as indeed they must be—melded together.

This means a different balance between standardization and flexibility, however, for different parts of the manufacturing process. An "average" balance across the plant will do nothing very well. If imposed throughout the line, it will simply result in high rigidity and big costs for the entire process, which is apparently what happened at GM. What is required is a reorganization of the process into modules, each with its own optimal balance.

Moreover, the relationships between these modules may have to change whenever the product, process, or distribution changes. Switching from selling heavy equipment to leasing it, for instance, may drastically change the ratio between finished-product output and spare-parts output. Or a fairly minor model change may alter the sequence in which major parts are assembled into the finished product. There is nothing very new in this, of course. But under the traditional line structure, such changes are ignored, or they take forever to accomplish. With competition intensifying and product life cycles shortening all the time, such changes cannot be ignored, and they have to be done fast. Hence the flotilla's modular organization.

But this organization requires more than a fairly drastic change in the factory's physical structure. It requires, above all, different communication and information. In the traditional plant, each sector and department reports separately upstairs. And it reports what upstairs has asked for. In the factory of 1999, sectors and departments will have to think through what information they owe to whom and what information they need from whom. A good deal of this information will flow sideways and across department lines, not upstairs. The factory of 1999 will be an information network.

Consequently, all the managers in a plant will have to know and understand the entire process, just as the destroyer commander has to know and understand the tactical plan of the entire flotilla. In the factory of 1999, managers will have to

Today's factory is a battleship. Tomorrow's will be a flotilla.

think and act as team members, mindful of the performance of the whole. Above all, they will have to ask: What do the people running the other modules need to know about the characteristics, the capacity, the plans, and the performance of *my* unit? And what, in turn, do we in my module need to know about theirs?

The last of the new concepts transforming manufacturing is systems design, in which the whole of manufacturing is seen as an integrated process that converts materials into goods, that is, into economic satisfactions.

Marks & Spencer, the British retail chain, designed the first such system in the 1930s. Marks & Spencer designs and tests the goods (whether textiles or foods) it has decided to sell. It designates one manufacturer to make each product under contract. It works with the manufacturer to produce the right merchandise with the right quality at the right price. Finally, it organizes just-in-time delivery of the finished products to its stores. The entire process is governed by a meticulous forecast as to when the goods will move off store shelves and into customers' shopping bags. In the last ten years or so, such systems management has become common in retailing.

> **Henry Ford did not build a system at River Rouge. He built an unwieldy monster.**

Though systems organization is still rare in manufacturing, it was actually first attempted there. In the early 1920s, when the Model T was in its full glory, Henry Ford decided to control the entire process of making and moving all the supplies and parts needed by his new plant, the gigantic River Rouge. He built his own steel mill and glass plant. He founded plantations in Brazil to grow rubber for tires. He bought the railroad that brought supplies to River Rouge and carried away the finished cars. He even toyed with the idea of building his own service centers nationwide and staffing them with mechanics trained in Ford-owned schools. But Ford conceived of all this as a financial edifice held together by ownership. Instead of building a system, he built a conglomerate, an unwieldy monster that was expensive, unmanageable, and horrendously unprofitable.

In contrast, the new manufacturing system is not "controlled" at all. Most of its parts are independent—independent suppliers at one end, customers at the other. Nor is it plant centered, as Ford's organization was. The new system sees the plant as little more than a wide place in the manufacturing stream. Planning and scheduling start with shipment to the final customer, just as they do at Marks & Spencer. Delays, halts, and redundancies have to be designed into the system—a warehouse here, an extra supply of parts and tools there, a stock of old products that are no longer being made but are still occasionally demanded by the market. These are necessary imperfections in a continuous flow that is governed and directed by information.

What has pushed American manufacturers into such systems design is the trouble they encountered when they copied Japan's just-in-time methods for supplying plants with materials and parts. The trouble could have been predicted, for the Japanese scheme is founded in social and logistic conditions unique to that country and unknown in the United States. Yet the shift seemed to American manufacturers a matter of procedure, indeed, almost trivial. Company after company found, however, that just-in-time delivery of supplies and parts created turbulence throughout their plants. And while no one could figure out what the problem was, the one thing that became clear was that with just-in-time deliveries, the plant no longer functions as a step-by-step process that begins at the receiving dock and ends when finished goods move into the shipping room. Instead, the plant must be redesigned from the end backwards and managed as an integrated flow.

Manufacturing experts, executives, and professors have urged such an approach for two or three decades now. And some industries, such as petroleum refining and large-scale construction, do practice it. But by and large, American and European manufacturing plants are neither systems designed nor systems managed. In fact, few companies have enough knowledge about what goes on in their plants to run them as systems. Just-in-time delivery, however, forces managers to ask systems questions: Where in the plant do we need redundancy? Where should we place the burden of adjustments? What costs should we incur in one place to minimize delay, risk, and vulnerability in another?

> **Producing does not stop when the product leaves the factory. Distribution and service are integral parts of the process.**

A few companies are even beginning to extend the systems concept of manufacturing beyond the plant and into the marketplace. Caterpillar, for instance, organizes its manufacturing to supply any replacement part anywhere in the world within 48 hours. But companies like this are still exceptions; they must become the rule. As soon as we define manufacturing as the process that converts things into economic satisfactions, it becomes clear that producing does not stop when the product leaves the factory. Physical distribution and product service are still part of the production process and should be integrated with it, coordinated with it, managed together with it. It is already widely recognized that servicing the product must be a major consideration during its design and production. By 1999, systems manufacturing will have an increasing influence on how we design and remodel plants and on how we manage manufacturing businesses.

Traditionally, manufacturing businesses have been organized "in series," with functions such as engineering, manufacturing, and marketing as successive steps. These days, that system is often complemented by a parallel team organization (Procter & Gamble's product management teams are a well-known example), which brings various functions together from the inception of a new product or process project. If manufacturing is a system, however, every decision in a manufacturing business becomes a manufacturing decision. Every decision should meet manufacturing's requirements and needs and in turn should exploit the strengths and capabilities of a company's particular manufacturing system.

When Honda decided six or seven years ago to make a new, upscale car for the U.S. market, the most heated strategic debate was not about design, performance, or price. It was about whether to distribute the Acura through Honda's well-established dealer network or to create a new market segment by building separate Acura dealerships at high cost and risk. This was a marketing issue, of course. But the decision was made by a team of design, engineering, manufacturing, and marketing people. And what tilted the balance toward the separate dealer network was a manufacturing consideration: the design for which independent distribution and service made most sense was the design that best utilized Honda's manufacturing capabilities.

Full realization of the systems concept in manufacturing is years away. It may not require a new Henry Ford. But it will certainly require very different management and very different managers. Every manager in tomorrow's manufacturing business will have to know and understand the manufacturing system. We might well adopt the Japanese custom of starting all new management people in the plant and in manufacturing jobs for the first few years of their careers. Indeed, we might go even further and require managers throughout the company to rotate into factory assignments throughout their careers — just as army officers return regularly to troop duty.

In the new manufacturing business, manufacturing is the integrator that ties everything together. It creates the economic value that pays for everything and everybody. Thus the greatest impact of the manufacturing systems concept will not be on the production process. As with SQC, its greatest impact will be on social and human concerns — on career ladders, for instance, or more important, on the transformation of *functional* managers into *business* managers, each with a specific role, but all members of the same production and the same cast. And surely, the manufacturing businesses of tomorrow will not be run by financial executives, marketers, or lawyers inexperienced in manufacturing, as so many U.S. companies are today.

There are important differences among these four concepts. Consider, for instance, what each means by "the factory." In SQC, the factory is a place where people work. In management accounting and the flotilla concept of flexible manufacturing, it is a place where work is being done — it makes no difference whether by people, by white mice, or

Caterpillar organizes its manufacturing to supply any part anywhere in the world within 48 hours.

by robots. In the systems concept, the factory is not a place at all; it is a stage in a process that adds economic value to materials. In theory, at least, the factory cannot and certainly should not be designed, let alone built, until the entire process of "making"—

> **Understand the "making" process all the way to the final customer. Then design and build the factory.**

all the way to the final customer—is understood. Thus defining the factory is much more than a theoretical or semantic exercise. It has immediate practical consequences on plant design, location, and size; on what activities are to be brought together in one manufacturing complex; even on how much and in what to invest.

Similarly, each of these concepts reflects a particular mind-set. To apply SQC, you don't have to think, you have to do. Management accounting concentrates on technical analysis, while the flotilla concept focuses on organization design and work flow. In the systems concept, there is great temptation to keep on thinking and never get to the doing. Each concept has its own tools, its own language, and addresses different people.

Nevertheless, what these four concepts have in common is far more important than their differences. Nowhere is this more apparent than in their assumption that the manufacturing process is a configuration, a whole that is greater than the sum of its parts. Traditional approaches all see the factory as a collection of individual machines and individual operations. The nineteenth century factory was an assemblage of machines. Taylor's scientific management broke up each job into individual operations and then put those operations together into new and different jobs. "Modern" twentieth century concepts—the assembly line and cost accounting—define performance as the sum of lowest cost operations. But none of the new concepts is much concerned with performance of the parts. Indeed, the parts as such can only underperform. The process produces results.

Management also will reflect this new perspective. SQC is the most nearly conventional in its implications for managers, since it does not so much change their job as shift much of it to the work force. But even managers with no business responsibility (and under SQC, plant people have none) will have to manage with an awareness of business considerations well beyond the plant. And every manufacturing manager will be responsible for integrating people, materials, machines, and time. Thus every manufacturing manager ten years hence will have to learn and practice a discipline that integrates engineering, management of people, and business economics into the manufacturing process. Quite a few manufacturing people are doing this already, of course—though usually unaware that they are doing something new and different. Yet such a discipline has not been systematized and is still not taught in engineering schools or business schools.

These four concepts are synergistic in the best sense of this much-abused term. Together—but only together—they tackle the conflicts that have most troubled traditional, twentieth century mass-production plants: the conflicts between people and machines, time and money, standardization and flexibility, and functions and systems. The key is that every one of these concepts defines performance as productivity and conceives of manufacturing as the physical process that adds economic value to materials. Each tries to provide economic value in a different way. But they share the same theory of manufacturing.

Author's note: I wish to acknowledge gratefully the advice and criticism I received on this piece from Bela Gold and Joseph Maciariello, friends and colleagues at the Claremont Graduate School.

Postindustrial manufacturing

Ramchandran Jaikumar

As global competition grows ever fiercer in manufacturing industries, American managers are adopting a new battle cry: "Beat 'em with technology or move – over there." Indeed, since 1975, the boom in information-intensive processing technologies has been explosive. A close look at how U.S. managers are actually using these technologies, however, silences their battle cry in a hurry. Yes, they are buying the hardware of flexible automation – but they are using it very poorly. Rather than narrowing the competitive gap with Japan, the technology of automation is widening it further.

> *"Flexible automation shifts the arena of competition from manufacturing to engineering."*

With few exceptions, the flexible manufacturing systems installed in the United States show an astonishing lack of flexibility. In many cases, they perform worse than the conventional technology they replace. The technology itself is not to blame; it is management that makes the difference. Compared with Japanese systems, those in U.S. plants produce an order-of-magnitude less variety of parts. Furthermore, they cannot run untended for a whole shift, are not integrated with the rest of their factories, and are less reliable. Even the good ones form, at best, a small oasis in a desert of mediocrity.

Lest this sound unduly harsh, consider the facts summarized in *Exhibit I*. In 1984 I conducted a focused study of 35 flexible manufacturing systems (FMSs) in the United States and 60 in Japan, a sample that represented more than half the installed systems in both countries. The kinds of products they made – large housings, crankcases, and the like – were comparable in size and complexity, and required similar metal-cutting times, numbers of tools, and precision of parts. The U.S. systems had an average of seven machines and the Japanese, six.

Here the similarities end. The average number of parts made by an FMS in the United States was 10; in Japan the average was 93, almost ten times greater. Seven of the U.S. systems made just 3 parts. The U.S. companies used FMSs the wrong way – for high-volume production of a few parts rather than for high-variety production of many parts at low cost per unit. Thus the annual volume per part in the United States was 1,727; in Japan, only 258. Nor have U.S. installations exploited opportunities to introduce new products. For every new part introduced into a U.S. system, 22 parts were introduced in Japan. In the critical metal-working industries, from which these numbers

Mr. Jaikumar, an associate professor at the Harvard Business School, focuses his research and teaching on the management of advanced manufacturing technologies. Before joining the faculty, he worked for ten years in industry, designing and implementing computer-integrated manufacturing and logistics systems. For his work he has twice been awarded the Management Science Prize for Practice, in 1976 and 1983.

Exhibit I	Comparison of FMSs studied in the United States and Japan	
	United States	Japan
System development time years	2.5 to 3	1.25 to 1.75
Number of machines per system	7	6
Types of parts produced per system	10	93
Annual volume per part	1,727	258
Number of parts produced per day	88	120
Number of new parts introduced per year	1	22
Number of systems with untended operations	0	18
Utilization rate* two shifts	52 %	84 %
Average metal-cutting time per day hours	8.3	20.2

*Ratio of actual metal-cutting time to time available for metal cutting.

come, the United States is not using manufacturing technology effectively. Japan is.

I have spent several years examining the experiences of companies that have installed FMSs. (See the insert entitled "Primary Research" for details of the study.) The object has been to observe the most sophisticated form of information-intensive technology in manufacturing. Flexible systems resemble miniature factories in operation. They are natural laboratories in which to study computer-integrated manufacturing, which is rapidly becoming the battleground for manufacturing supremacy around the globe.

The battle is on, and the United States is losing badly. It may even lose the war if it doesn't soon figure out how better to use the new technology of automation for competitive advantage. This does not mean investing in more equipment; in today's manufacturing environment, it is how the equipment is used that is important. Success comes from achieving continuous process improvement through organizational learning and experimentation.

Technology leadership

The FMS installations surveyed in *Exhibit I* were, as noted, technically alike. They had similar machines and did similar types of work. The difference in results was mainly due to the extent of the installed base of machinery, the work force's technical literacy, and management's competence. In each of these areas, Japan was far ahead of the United States.

In the last five years, Japan has outspent the United States two to one in automation. During that time, 55% of the machine tools introduced in Japan were computer numerically controlled (CNC) machines, key parts of FMSs. In the United States, the figure was only 18%. Of all these machines installed worldwide since 1975, more than 40% are in Japan. What's more, over two-thirds of the CNC machines in Japan went to small and medium-sized companies.

Just counting how much of this technology companies use is not enough. Because software development lies at the heart of this increasingly information-intensive manufacturing process, the technological literacy of a company's workers is critical. In the Japanese companies I studied, more than 40% of the work force was made up of college-educated engineers, and all had been trained in the use of CNC machines. In the U.S. companies studied, only 8% of the workers were engineers, and less than 25% had been trained on CNC machines. Training to upgrade skills was 3 times longer in Japan than in the United States. Compared with U.S. plants, Japanese factories had an average of 2½ times as many CNC machines, 4 times as many engineers, and 4 times as many people trained to use the machines.

Management's role

A skilled work force and a large installed base of equipment build the foundation for technological leadership. It is the competence of managers, however, that makes such leadership happen. To understand why, we should look more closely at recent experience with FMS technology.

A flexible manufacturing system is a computer-controlled grouping of semi-independent work stations linked by automated material-handling systems. The purpose of an FMS is to manufacture efficiently several kinds of parts at low to medium volumes. All activities in the system—metal cutting, monitoring tool wear, moving parts from one machine to another, setup, inspection, tool adjustment, material handling, scheduling, and dispatching—are under pre-

> ## Primary research
>
> The research on which this article is based took three years and included the detailed study of 95 flexible manufacturing systems in the United States and Japan—more than half the installed FMSs at the time. I examined published and company records of all these installations, held long interviews with managers and system designers, and observed the systems in operation. I had two goals: first, to obtain an overview of the use of the systems, their capabilities, and where they succeed and fail; and second, to understand why and how the successful ones work.
>
> My choice of sites for the second part of this study reflected stringent conditions: all had to be in the same industry, the companies had to have a history of success with two or more systems, and the systems had to influence more than one FMS cell.
>
> Only the machine tool industry in Japan met all these conditions. My choice was especially fortunate in that it is the mother industry for creating capital goods. Machine tool producers use their own products, and their process innovations quickly lead to product development in other areas. Further, the industry is fragmented; most companies are small and family owned. Because the U.S. metal-working industry is structurally similar to the machine tool industry in Japan (more than three-quarters of manufacturing output in the United States comes from operations with fewer than 50 people), my findings bear directly on how these technologies would affect most U.S. manufacturers.
>
> Between 1972 and 1984, 23 companies in Japan built flexible manufacturing systems. Of these, 6 were nonmachine tool companies that wanted them for in-house use. The remaining 17 were machine tool companies; 16 built systems for their own use, 9 built systems for other companies, and 8 sold more than 2 systems. I visited 7 of these companies, including the only 3 that had fully automated factories, and examined in detail the operations of 22 systems.

cise computer control. In operation, an FMS is a miniature automated factory.

The system at one prominent Midwestern heavy-equipment producer consisted of 12 machines that made just 8 different parts for a total volume of 5,000 units a year. Once the FMS went on line, management prevented workers from making process improvements by encouraging them not to make any changes. "If it ain't broke, don't fix it" became the watchword.

The FMS boosted machine uptime and productivity, but it did not come close to realizing its full—and distinctive—strategic promise. The technology was applied in a way that ignored its huge potential for flexibility and for generating organizational learning.

Management treated the FMS as if it were just another set of machines for high-volume, standardized production—which is precisely what it is not. Captive to old-fashioned Taylorism and its principles of scientific management, these executives separated the establishment of procedures from their execution, replaced skilled blue-collar machinists with trained operators, and emphasized machine uptime and productivity. In short, they mastered narrow-purpose production on expensive FMS technology designed for high-powered, flexible usage.

This is no way to run a railroad. Certainly, Frederick W. Taylor's work still applies—but not to this environment. Managing an FMS as if it were the old Ford plant at River Rouge is worse than wrong; it is paralyzing. In this case there was little, if any, attention given to process or program flexibility and almost no support for software improvement. Management failed to utilize the FMS's improved capabilities, from which even greater improvements might have flowed over time.

Not surprisingly, the flexibility achieved by this FMS was much less than that of a stand-alone CNC machining center. And that's the *good* news. The system had four operators per shift, each of whom was responsible for checking gauges, changing hydraulic fluid and parts like drill bits, and making simple diagnoses when something went wrong. These tasks, as specified by management, were very procedural, and no operator had the discretion to change procedures. If anything, the complexity of the FMS forced operators to stick more rigidly to procedure than they did at the stand-alone CNC machining centers.

Goals for management

How, then, should managers look at FMSs? About what should they ask? For one thing, development time. The systems in the United States take $2^{1}/_{2}$ to 3 years and about 25,000 man-hours to conceive, develop, install, and get running. Japanese systems take $1^{1}/_{4}$ to $1^{3}/_{4}$ years and 6,000 man-hours. Here, again, the difference is management. U.S. project teams are usually large groups made up of specialists who design systems for a much greater level of flexibility than their companies are prepared to use. This greater complexity means that projects not only take longer but have plenty of bugs when finished. Delays create enormous pressure on software engineers to take shortcuts and seek hard-wired fixes.

At the end of a project, as a rule, the team is disbanded. The engineers assigned to maintain a system, who are usually not its developers, are reluctant to make any changes. They know about all the bugs but are unwilling to tinker with things because

Exhibit II	Comparison of Japanese FMSs with the systems they replaced	
	FMSs	Conventional systems
Number of parts produced per system*	182	182
Number of systems with untended operations	18	0
Number of machine tools	133	253
Number of operators three shifts	129	601
Utilization rate two shifts	84 %†	61 %

*To make the comparison useful, I have held the number of parts made by each system constant.

†For three shifts, the figure is 92%.

"you never know what may happen." The result: inflexibility.

By contrast, the FMS installations in Japan are remarkably flexible. This would not be so troublesome for the United States if the old-fashioned productivity of its systems, for which flexibility gets sacrificed, were better than that of Japanese systems. But it is not. The average utilization rate (metal-cutting time as a percentage of total time) of U.S. flexible manufacturing systems over two shifts was 52%, as opposed to 84% in Japan. Over three shifts, because of reliable untended operations, the figure in Japan was even higher.

Where does so huge a difference come from? In a word, the *reliability* designed into the system. In Japan, system designers strive to create operations that can run untended. Of the 60 FMSs I studied, 18 ran untended during the night shift. Such systems take more time and resources to develop than those that require even a single attendant, because designers have to anticipate all possible contingencies. But the additional costs are well worth it. So demanding a design objective leads in practice to a great deal of advance problem solving and process improvement. The entire project team remains with the system long after installation, continually making changes. Learning occurs throughout—and learning gets translated into ongoing process mastery and productivity enhancement. This learning is what gives rise to, and sustains, competitive advantage.

Most of the systems built in Japan after 1982 have achieved untended operations and system uptime of an astonishing 90% to 99%. Operators on the shop floor make continual programming changes and are responsible for writing new programs for both parts and systems as a whole. They are highly skilled engineers with multifunctional responsibilities. Like the designers, they work best in small teams. Most important, managers see FMS technology for what it is—flexible—and create operating objectives and protocols that capitalize on this special capability. Not bound by outdated mass-production assumptions, they view the challenge of flexible manufacturing as automating a job shop, not simply making a transfer line flexible. The difference in results is enormous, but the the vision that leads to it is in human scale. No magic here—just an intelligent process of thinking through what new technology means for how work should be organized.

FMS on line

To find out more about this "job shop" approach, I examined more closely 22 FMS installations at Hitachi-Seiki, Yamazaki Mazak, Okuma, Murata, Mori-Seiki, Makino, and Fanuc. As *Exhibit II* shows, these systems far outperformed the conventional CNC equipment they replaced.

Both systems produced the same variety of parts. But the FMSs did it with five times fewer workers than the conventional systems. Moreover, it took only half as many flexible machines to produce the same volume of parts as conventional machines. The CNC machines used in both systems were identical; the FMSs, however, also employed robots, special material-handling equipment, automated storage systems, and tool-handling equipment. These support devices added another 30% to hardware costs, but they helped boost average uptime from 61% to 92% and made untended operations possible. These benefits alone more than justified the extra cost; better quality and reduced inventories were a bonus.

Potential FMS users often worry that the systems are difficult to justify strictly in economic terms. Based on the experiences of Japanese companies, these fears are groundless. All 22 systems I studied in Japan met their companies' ROI criterion of a three-year payback.

Even so, the impact of flexible manufacturing on the performance of a company reaches far beyond simple productivity rates and investment calculations. FMSs take on strategic importance when the installed base of flexible systems in a factory reaches a critical mass. Only when separate "islands of automation" in a plant start to link does management realize the possibilities for new kinds of competitive advantage via manufacturing.

Of the six Japanese companies that used flexible automation extensively, three had fully automated fabrication plants. At the time I visited them, they were the only flexible manufacturing factories in the world. Their productivity was stupendous.

Exhibit III compares the performance of one such factory before and after the introduction of total flexible automation, and *Exhibit IV* shows the effect of such performance on cost structure and competition in an industry. Specifically, the exhibit compares the manpower requirements of various manufacturing systems for metal-cutting operations: if it took 100 people in a conventional Japanese factory to make a certain number of machine parts, it would take 194 people in a conventional U.S. factory—but only 43 in a Japanese FMS-equipped factory. If U.S. companies mastered flexible automation as the Japanese have, they would have more than a fourfold increase in labor productivity. This efficiency in labor is part of the reason that smaller companies in Japan have been able to use FMS technology so effectively.

Perhaps even more interesting than such aggregate improvements are their components. The largest manpower reduction in the exhibit is in manufacturing overhead, where an FMS cuts the number of workers from 64 to 5. In engineering, an FMS cuts the number of workers from 34 to 16. One consequence of these reductions (92% in manufacturing overhead, but only 53% in engineering) is to change the composition of the work force: engineers now outnumber production workers three to one. This may not sound like much at first, but it signals a fundamental change in the environment of manufacturing.

Flexible automation shifts the arena of competition from manufacturing to engineering, from running the plant to planning it. In the FMS environment, engineering innovation and engineering productivity hold the keys to success. Engineering now performs the critical line function. Manufacturing has become, by comparison, a staff or support function.

Managing above the line

Picture a "lights out" factory operating untended, with general-purpose CNC machines that make a wide variety of parts and are capable of adapting easily to new demands. If two such factories compete with similar products, competition will focus on price. This is so because all costs in the development of tools, fixtures, and programs are sunk before the first unit is produced. The only variable costs are those of materials and energy, which usually amount to less than 10% of total costs.

Exhibit III: Performance of one factory before and after automation

		Before	After
	Types of parts produced per month*	543	543
	Number of pieces produced per month*	11,120	11,120
	Floor space required	16,500 m²	6,600 m²
Equipment per system	CNC machine tools	66	38
	General-purpose machine tools	24	5
	Total	**90**	**43**
Personnel per system three shifts	Operators	170	36
	Distribution and production control workers	25	3
	Total	**195**	**39**
Average processing time per part† days	Machining time	35	3
	Unit assembly	14	7
	Final assembly	42	20
	Total	**91**	**30**

*To make the comparison useful, I have held these figures constant.
†This includes time spent in queue.

Exhibit IV: Manpower requirements for metal-cutting operations to make the same number of identical parts

	Conventional systems		FMSs
	United States	Japan	Japan
Engineering	34	18	16
Manufacturing overhead	64	22	5
Fabrication	52	28	6
Assembly	44	32	16
Total number of workers	**194**	**100**	**43**

Note: There is no column here for FMSs in the United States because, at the time of this study, no domestic machine tool producer had an FMS on line.

Exhibit V — Degree of automation in production activities of 20 Japanese FMSs
in numbers of systems

	Metal-cutting operations	Material handling		Setup		Process control*	Production control		Inventory management	
		Parts	Tools	Parts	Tools		Planning	Dispatching	Parts	Tools
Manual	–	–	–	16	13	–	4	–	–	–
Manual with computer assistance	–	–	–	2	–	–	5	–	–	–
Automated with manual override	2	–	–	–	2	–	10	–	–	15
Untended†	18	20	20	2	5	20	1	20	20	5

*Tool monitoring, inspection, and feedback.

†To qualify as untended, a system had to run without manual assistance for one shift a day and have a 98% utilization rate.

Exhibit VI — Production activities in an average FMS in Japan*

	Metal-cutting operations	Material handling		Setup		Process control	Production control		Inventory management		Total
		Parts	Tools	Parts	Tools		Planning	Dispatching	Parts	Tools	
Average system losses as a percentage of total time	1.6 %	5 %	–	–	5 %	2 %	–	3 %	–	–	16.6 %†
Manual labor time per system hours	2	–	–	11	7	3	2.5	.5	–	–	26

*An average FMS in Japan has six machines, creating a total of 144 hours of available metal-cutting time per day.

†This figure seems to imply that the system's utilization rate over three shifts would be 83.4%, not 92% as asserted in Exhibit II. There is no discrepancy; the figures don't match because problems in some areas, such as material handling, cause system losses that do not result in machine downtime.

Each factory's profits will erode over time as other companies acquire the same operating capabilities. How, then, would a company stay ahead? One way is by creating new physical assets in the form of better programmed and better managed equipment. Each plant's competitive fate would rest heavily on its ability to create facilities that generate performance advantages—and to do it faster than the competition. When the lion's share of costs are sunk before production starts, the creation and management of intellectual assets becomes the prime task of management.

This is manufacturing's new competitive environment. It may sound like something from the distant future, but the Japanese are doing it now. The crucial variable in this kind of environment is automation—the ability of an FMS to run untended. And Japanese manufacturing companies are becoming increasingly expert in that field.

Exhibit V summarizes my findings from 20 of the 22 Japanese FMSs on the extraordinary degree of automation reflected in different production activities. *Exhibit VI* presents data from these 20 systems on the amount of manual labor time spent on the factory floor to support such levels of automation. Average system losses took 16.6% of total operating time, about a third the figure in U.S. systems. Each 144 hours of metal-cutting time took only 26 hours of manual effort, which included direct labor as well as required activities usually associated with manufacturing overhead. In the United States, manufacturing overhead activities are separated from direct labor and take about ten times longer.

In most plants, 26 hours of manual effort translate into two workers per system for each of two shifts. In all 22 of these FMSs, however, there was a third person on each shift, whose work accounted for part of the 26 hours of manual effort. By dividing the work among three people, the companies that had these systems purposely created extra time for such process-improvement activities as additional test cutting of new parts, observing machine behavior, and examining statistics on performance. In all 22 systems, each of the workers did these nonrequired—but immensely valuable—tasks. The number of people required to do all this in conventional systems making the same parts in the same companies was four times greater.

The distribution of the 26 hours of manual effort is also instructive. More than half were spent loading and unloading pallets. The other major activity, which took 7 hours, was mounting tools and qualifying them on machines. Together, these efforts accounted for 80% of the time spent on manual labor. Workers loaded pallets and mounted tools during the day shift, and the machines ran untended at night. Production planning, a weekly activity, took only one hour of a person's time. Systems making a large variety of parts also had automated methods for production planning. Those with a low variety of parts did it manually.

The FMS installations performed exceptionally well. Delivery performance in each system, tracked during a three-month period, was 100%. The high reliability of individual machines and of the system itself kept the variance in unscheduled downtime to only 2%. The scheduled slack for software testing and process experiments ranged from 4% to 9% of capacity and was more than enough to accommodate any variation in machine reliability. Each system met its production schedule, as long as the schedule observed the constraints of capacity. In addition, only six pieces in a thousand had a quality problem. Of these, three were reworked, usually by the operators themselves. The other three were scrapped. Tool breakage caused most of these quality problems, and the machine operators could make the necessary adjustments.

With such impressive levels of performance, few contingencies demanded management's attention. In fact, executives were largely absent from day-to-day operations. Instead of concerning themselves with internal operations, they focused their attention on how to meet competitive pressures on product performance. In the United States, on the other hand, managers spend so much time on routine problems with quality and production delivery schedules that they have virtually no time left over to plan for long-term process improvement.

As noted before, the prime task of management once the system has been made reliable is not to categorize tasks or regiment workers but to create the fixed assets—the systems and software—needed to make products. This calls for intellectual assets, not just pieces of hardware. Thus the new role of management in manufacturing is to create and nurture the project teams whose intellectual capabilities produce competitive advantage. What gets managed is intellectual capital, not equipment.

The technology of flexible manufacturing has led managers into a drastically altered competitive landscape. This new landscape has a number of important features:

> A sharp focus on intellectual assets as the basis for a company's distinctive competence.
>
> A heightened emphasis on the selection of the portfolio of projects a company chooses to manage.
>
> A close attention to the market and to the special competence of process engineers.
>
> A steady adjustment of product mix and price in order to maintain full capacity utilization.
>
> A pointed emphasis on reducing fixed manufacturing costs and the time required to generate new products, processes, and programs.
>
> An intensification of cost-based competition for manufactured products.

I am convinced that the heart of this new manufacturing landscape is the management of manufacturing projects: selecting them, creating teams to work on them, and managing workers' intellectual development. In company after company in Japan, systems engineers with a thorough knowledge of several disciplines have proved the key to the success of flexible manufacturing systems. One rigidly organized Japanese company, recognizing the importance of such versatile teams, now rotates experienced engineers through all manufacturing departments. Another, which already had job rotation, has begun to keep its engineers longer in each area so they can learn more from their FMS experience.

In contrast with the traditional Japanese approach of involving a large number of people in decision making, small teams of highly competent, engineering-oriented people have been most successful with flexible manufacturing. These groups have succeeded because they are given responsibility for both design and operations. They remain on a project until the FMS achieves 90% uptime and untended operations. Perhaps most important, in all the Japanese companies I studied, the teams came entirely from engineering and were given line responsibility for day-to-day operations.

New mission statement

The management of FMS technology is taking place in a different manufacturing environment, and thus consists of new imperatives:

Build small, cohesive teams. Very small groups of highly skilled generalists show a remarkable propensity to succeed.

Manage process improvement, not just output. FMS technology fundamentally alters the economics of production by drastically reducing variable labor costs. When these costs are low, little can be gained by reducing them further. The challenge is to develop and manage physical and intellectual assets, not the production of goods. Choosing projects that develop intellectual and physical assets is more important than monitoring the costs of day-to-day operations. Old-fashioned, sweat-of-the-brow manufacturing effort is now less important than system design and team organization.

Broaden the role of engineering management to include manufacturing. The use of small, technologically proficient teams to design, run, and improve FMS operations signals a shift in focus from managing people to managing knowledge, from controlling variable costs to managing fixed costs, and from production planning to project selection. This shift gives engineering the line responsibilities that have long been the province of manufacturing.

Treat manufacturing as a service. In an untended FMS environment, all of the tools and software programs required to make a part have to be created before the first unit is produced. While the same is true of typical parts and assembly operations, the difference in an FMS is that there are no allowances for in-the-line, people-intensive adjustments. As a result, competitive success increasingly depends on management's ability to anticipate and respond quickly to changing market needs. With FMS technology, even a small, specialized operation can accommodate shifts in demand. Manufacturing now responds much like a professional service industry, customizing its offerings to the preferences of special market segments.

Making flexibility and responsiveness the mission of manufacturing flies in the face of Taylor's view of the world, which for 75 years has shaped thinking about manufacturing. FMS technology points inevitably toward a new managerial ethos—an ethos dedicated to the building of knowledge in the flexible service of markets, not merely to the building of things. Scale is no longer the central concern. Size no longer provides barriers to entry. The minimum efficient scale for FMS operations is a cell of roughly six machines and fewer than a half a dozen people. That's the new reality.

Going to FMS-based operations does *not* require lots of money or people. It can be done—at its best, it *is* done—on a small scale. The critical ingredient here is nothing other than the competence of a small group of people. There is no Eastern mystery in this, no secrets known only to the Japanese. We can do it too—if we will.

What, after all, is a manufacturing company? Today, no artist would represent a factory as a huge, austere building with bellowing smokestacks. The behemoth is gone. The efficient factory is now an aggregation of small cells of electronically linked and controlled FMSs. New technology enables these operating cells to be combined in nonlinear ways. No shared base of infrastructure mandates large-scale production integration. The days of Taylor's immense, linear production systems are largely gone.

Unless U.S. managers understand the implications of Japan's mastery of FMS technology, their companies will fall further behind. Flexible manufacturing systems are no longer a theory, a pipe dream. They exist. And the leverage they provide on continuous process improvement is immense. Making automation work means a whole new level of process mastery. A large number of Japanese factories demonstrate its reality every day. They lead the way; we linger behind at our own peril.

*For some U.S. companies,
computer-integrated manufacturing is the only way
to justify staying in a business.*

A CEO's Common Sense of CIM: An Interview with J. Tracy O'Rourke

by Bernard Avishai

According to Wickham Skinner ("What Matters to Manufacturing," HBR January-February 1988), too many managers now approach production difficulties with "a menu of textbook techniques"—CIM, for example—when they should be thinking through the same old questions: What is my business? Where is the market? What machines and flexibilities do I really need?

With Skinner's strictures in mind, HBR turned to J. Tracy O'Rourke, CEO of Allen-Bradley and one of America's leading authorities on computer-integrated manufacturing. Allen-Bradley, a subsidiary of Rockwell International Corporation, manufactures industrial automation controls and systems. In 1983, the company formed a CIM task force to manufacture motor contactors—a device that turns motors on and off—conforming to world standards. A fully computer-integrated contactor plant was in operation in Milwaukee by 1986. Today the line produces 600 units per hour in any of more than 777 variations and in lot sizes as small as one or two.

Mr. O'Rourke, a mechanical engineer with nearly 30 years of executive and entrepreneurial experience, joined Allen-Bradley in 1978. He has been president of the company since 1981 and in 1986 was appointed CEO.

The interview was conducted at HBR offices by Bernard Avishai, associate editor.

HBR: *You have been described as an evangelist for computer-integrated manufacturing. Are you?*

O'Rourke: No, I'm a businessman, a shrewd one, I hope. You know, people were running around five or six years ago saying that we were going to have this big, technological industrial revolution. We had hit on computer-driven manufacturing solutions that were way ahead of the problems they were meant to solve. I kept saying, "Who's going to make a revolution? I can't figure out how we'll do it. For God's sake, where are the experienced, trained people going to come from?"

Besides, there's no reason why the manager of a company would wake up one Monday morning and say, "Computer-integrated manufacturing is my goal." Computer automation is a means, not an end in itself. Managers plan for the future: "This is the business I want to be in. Here's the competitive situation today, and here's the likely competitive situation tomorrow." Then they ask, "How do I design products, develop and manufacture products, sell and service products to stay competitive—catch up if I'm behind, stay ahead if I'm ahead?"

Why CIM, then?

If you're behind the world competition, apply to manufacturing the best technology you can. The Chinese pay workers $25 a month. American companies cannot have as many workers as the Chinese do. It's just common sense. And the Chinese buy raw materials like oil and copper on the same world market we do, at the same price. So access to cheaper materials is no longer a weapon against countries with cheap labor. It leads you to conclude that computer automation is our only weapon.

How did computer automation become your weapon?

We didn't get up one morning five years ago with a desire to build a CIM plant. To change in just one step to a peopleless, paperless environment—are you kidding? But we had a competitive situation that was biting at us.

Foreign competitors were making contactors that conformed to International Electro-Technical Commission (IEC) specifications—contactors, the little ones, which did essentially the same job as the great big black ones that we made. Obviously the little ones were in material alone about one-third the cost of the big ones—not a serious problem to us as long as Americans were making most of their own machinery and using it here. Our customers seemed to think that those little "flimsy" IEC things were something that people in Europe used because they couldn't afford something good.

Anyway, American manufacturers began to import a lot of machines, and they were delivered with those damn little switches on. People found that, for most commercial applications, they worked just fine. So suddenly we were put on the defensive. And we had put our stake in the ground, selling programmable controllers for electric motors worldwide, 100 million to 200 million a year outside the United States. We thought, what the hell, if we've got to play defense we may as well play offense too and design contactors so that we could sell them worldwide.

Why did you choose advanced manufacturing over other ways to compete?

We didn't, not at first. We did the easy things. We went out and tried to buy somebody. There wasn't anybody to buy. We tried to license the products, then looked for a joint venture, but we couldn't find a partner. Of course, during this time we learned a lot about the cost structure of the industry. And we discovered something peculiar. In Australia, the identical contactor would sell for $8, in Germany for $16. Identical—form, fit, and function.

I told my people, "Look, if it sells in Australia for $8, someday it's going to sell for that worldwide. You don't pay twice as much just because you're in America." So we had to design a product that could meet the quality standards and make a profit at $8. My people shrugged their shoulders and said, "Well, no big problem."

Presumably, there were problems at $8.

Yes there were. We did a little pilot plant, with some fairly hard automation—fully operator-assisted machines, little subassemblies, a little cell, fairly integrated. People would come in and say, "Wow! Isn't that modern." And it was. And then we ran the numbers and found that we would *absolutely* lose our shirt. Even if we eliminated all the direct labor, 100% of it, we still would not be able to make money at eight bucks a piece.

That's fine, I said, we won't go into the business. The hell with it. We'll just battle them at the beaches. Slowly but surely, they will take market share. But I am not going to fund this thing. Imagine, $5 million to design the product and about $15 million to tool the plant, and we still would not make any money at all.

What changed your mind?

Some of our hot-shots researched the thing further. We found that if we had a totally paperless, peopleless environment, and on top of that, if we could end up at the end of every day with *no inventory*, we could justify the investment. And I said, hell, that sounds great. We've been going around telling our customers that plants like this are technically possible. Why don't we get our geniuses down in Cleveland to propose a system?

They costed it all out and said, "We can bring it in somewhere between $15 million and $20 million." It looked good on paper; it took a year's work.

Did you have particular trouble justifying such a futuristic factory to your financial officers?

My financial people were going crazy. But then, look at the crazy financial models they've been using to justify capital investments on products. There's nothing wrong with saying, "Someday, I want to make my money back. Sooner or later I've got to get a greater return than my cost of capital." Good Lord, if you didn't believe that, why would you be a capitalist?

But the old financial models have failed manufacturing companies. Return on investment, internal rate of return—such abstractions focus on the time-value of money and give little consideration to the strategic opportunities and threats presented by technological advance. They make no sense when applied to manufacturing systems that aren't junked when the product lines are. Besides, some of CIM's most valued benefits are simply not quantifiable. How do you put a price on corporate learning?

Give us an example of failing models.

A classic case is in the metal-working industry, which still uses "full absorption accounting": direct labor is generally used to absorb overhead charges.

> "My financial people were going crazy. 'A factory without inventory? You'll get laughed out of the room.'"

But today direct labor accounts for less than 10% of a product's sales value, and CIM can lower that percentage even further. So obviously, measuring costs based on labor's absorption of overhead is nonsense. Accounting has to distinguish between those expenditures that add value and those that only add cost.

Anyway, the old investment models were developed to compare one project with another. They were not developed to be an aid to strategic thinking. If I have five guys who are equally honest, and the revenue line is honest, and the cost line is honest, and the capital is honest—and I have to choose two projects out of five—then I just put all the data into the computer and out squirts the numbers that show which project to choose. Zap.

But what if the projects are not all of the same strategic importance? What if one project is crucial to the long-term qualifications of your personnel? We begin to get lazy about such hard decisions—"risk averse," as the academics say.

Still, people had reason to be skeptical of CIM.

Well, they looked at you strange. When I came to Allen-Bradley, we had 365 days of inventory. Can you picture that? And top management thought it was fine. Private company, plenty of money. We had beat it down to about 110 days over 10 years. But this was different. "You mean, Tracy, you're going to go to the board of directors and tell them that one of the ways you justify this thing is having *no* inventory? You'll get laughed out of the room."

Well, it wasn't going to pencil out any other way. If we'd have had this $15 million investment in traditional manufacturing, $15 million worth of inventory in finished goods and materials would have been the killer. Anyway, we *knew* how to run that system with no inventory. It was simply a matter of planning from the top down and building from the bottom up—developing the product and process simultaneously.

Were there other reasons for skepticism?

Actually, the thing that rattled most people was quality. We have had a very low reject rate in our electromechanical products—3½% of sales. That included prevention, inspection, scrap, rework, and warranty. But the people who designed the contactor line said, "Look, if we have to design this thing as precisely as the process engineers tell us we have to, and if we're going to computer-model everything, we know everything's got to fit together before we ever build a single contactor. Let's assume that we'll have no rejects."

Now, clearly, perfection is never absolute. But you can design a product and put it together so that rejects are, in effect, a thing of the past—which is what I told my wonderful board of directors. Well, if I hadn't completely lost my credibility with them by that point, I might have then.

By the way, our estimates turned out to be rather conservative. The plant was brought in for $15 million. We have no inventory. We're not even tempted to build it; the plant is so responsive and so fast that

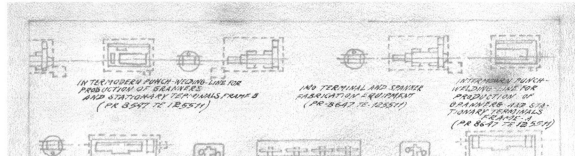

there's no reason to have it. As for quality, our reject rates are 15 parts per million.

You didn't know things would turn out so well at the start, surely. How did you manage the risks?

True, but there was no capricious thinking. We did an in-depth risk analysis. The high risk, we concluded, was not in the machines. It was not in designing the contactor. It was not in getting the parts to fit together: robots could put parts together. The risk was in managing the software, in integrating our information system with our control system. That had never been done.

At first I said, whoops, that's too big a risk. But some of my people came up with a way that loosely couples the information system to the control system on the machines. In fact, we started on our plant without knowing precisely how the information system would be working. Within about six months, they had the information system and the control system all integrated.

This may be a difficult concept to grasp. What do you mean by "managing software"?

Every computer-driven manufacturing system is governed by two kinds of software: the information system, which tells the machines *what* to build, and the control system, which tells the machines *how* to build—and tracks quality. The question is, what information has to be known in real time? How much of the computer's precious memory should we devote to what?

Now, when you try to put in the information system simultaneously with the control system, the former has a lot of problems. Let's say a contactor base comes to station one. The computer reads the bar code that we stick on the bottom of the base and then goes back to the information system—which governs orders and schedule—to find out exactly what kind of thing to build, how many, and so on. If the control software—"build like this," "inspect for that"—was not properly separated from and integrated with information software, God knows how long that base would sit there. It could sit for five minutes. You can waste a whole bunch of the computer memory—and time—looking for where the hell the data is.

So we had to find a way to partition the software. Today it takes only six seconds for station one to know what to do. We still have got all those diagnostic things running, quality inspections—practically every kind of sensor you can think of operating in real time—3,500 automated test inspection stations.

Should you have tried to get software vendors to manage this problem for you?

If we'd have been able to go outside and hire somebody, we would have done that. We would have said,

> "The risk was in integrating our information system with our control system. That had never been done."

"Please, you do it, we'll write you a check." But we couldn't find anybody to do exactly what we wanted to do.

Still, it seems that grappling with software integration forced you to come up with an elegant solution. You don't seem to regret that there wasn't a vendor out there.

No, we don't regret it at all. But clearly, the cost of a commercially available package would have been a lot less than we spent. Somebody's had all the blood on the table, debugging the thing, getting it to work. Manufacturing companies really should take advantage of that.

For instance, we have a very effective statistical process-control package running locally through the system. Allen-Bradley happens to be in the business of developing and selling statistical process-control packages. Had we not been in that business, we would have just bought a package.

Had you resolved product quality problems before the problems of integration?

Absolutely. Automating a system that's out of whack can only give you automated confusion. Bad manufacturing practices or unstable processes shouldn't be automated. You wouldn't dream of putting your company's general ledger system under computer control if you couldn't balance it by hand.

Of course, when I use the word "quality," I mean it in a very broad sense. Not only did the precision of the components have to be at a higher level than we'd coped with before but we needed precision also in the way components were put together. Few people put springs into assemblies very well, for example. We had to design the product so that the springs could be put in from the side instead of the top. Bad quality is nothing but a series of small compromises.

In retrospect, are there product lines that are natural candidates for CIM?

There's no cookie-cutter answer. As in any business decision, you start with the question, "Should I be in this business or not?" In many cases, if you're completely honest with yourself, you'll do the shareholders a favor and get out.

Still, the best candidates are products that do not have to be enormously flexible, not products that have option on top of option. Then make sure you are not too far down the products' life cycles. You have to

> "We wanted to put the CIM plant where the union was, to prove that unions need not be an obstacle."

expect the demand to be steady for a while—time enough to master the technology. At the same time, if you're going to make this investment in programmable automation—which will be substantial—you have to believe that your system will have a longer life than the products the system was designed to build. These are not boat anchors you're buying. Unlike the products they make, these systems *are* flexible and reusable. You can't afford to throw them away when the product matures.

Is the company's design organization a natural candidate for computer integration?

Yes. Too many people think of the factory floor when they think of CIM. In fact, if you're going to be in the business of conceiving and designing products, the only sensible way today is to use every modern computer technique you can find, whether it's computer-aided design, computer-aided engineering, or product-function analysis. If you're not going to arm your engineers with the latest product-development systems, they will not be competitive.

Our contactor plant plans would have been impossible without computers. We modeled the product with computers. People who were experienced in machine assembly were teamed with the people who did the modeling. We simulated the machine, we simulated the part, and by the time we got the machine on the factory floor, the computers had put everything together in their little artificial minds.

How did you know your people were ready for CIM?

We were confident in our engineers. We're in the business. Our people were nearly ready. The odds are your people are not.

Take a look at the way most companies introduce computers into their offices. We're dropping all these microcomputers in front of everybody. But do we change their work routines? Oh sure, we use electronic mail. But we don't get nearly the productivity gains that we could if we linked everybody to the large data bases and taught workers how to use them.

None of this means your people aren't capable, intelligent, hard working. And I'm not saying, "Don't go ahead." You learn by doing. And people can get up to speed very fast. Their confidence builds quickly.

Are there any rules of thumb to help them along?

I've got ten rules that you really should abide by. Pick a project that will succeed, pick a project that

will succeed, and, three, pick a project that will succeed. I've got seven more.

I don't think you'll see many two-million-square-foot plants torn down and built back up. Serious

"Bringing that supplier in as a partner was key."

managers will pick departments to develop, they'll pick small plants, they'll pick parts of projects. They'll do the plant work, they'll do the engineering work, and then they'll integrate the plants.

What unexpected personnel problems cropped up at Allen-Bradley in getting your contactor plant into operation?

Well, let's say I didn't have any trouble finding a volunteer to manage it—once it was running. But at first nobody jumped up and ran to the front of the room and said, "I want to be the project leader who's going to manage this very complex development program."

We went to the vice president of operations in that product group. "Hey, we would like very much for you to be the project leader." He was extraordinarily flattered to be asked. That show of confidence was important. He's since led the project just wonderfully well as far as I'm concerned.

Did you get resistance from, say, hourly workers or unions?

On the contrary. We have 30-some plants, and only one that's unionized. We wanted to put the CIM plant where the union was, to prove that unions need not be an obstacle. Why offend workers who happen to belong to a union?

So we went to the union leadership. We explained that the engineers designing the product and the process, building the equipment—all of them—were right there. But we needed an agreement from the union to go ahead. First, that union leaders wouldn't oppose construction. Second, that they wouldn't go call a press conference or get on television or write the *Harvard Business Review* and condemn automation. We said, "If you want to go around and bad-mouth automation, it's perfectly all right with us. That's your God-given right. But don't bad-mouth this plant."

Then we told them that we wanted four hourly workers to come forward and go through very intense training as operators. We wanted to administer aptitude tests, not choose on the basis of seniority. We wanted those people to work with the machines as they were being built. We wanted them to commune with those machines. In the end, we selected two men, two women—one was a minority.

So the maintenance people, the machinery-building people, and the several operators are all part of the same bargaining unit. The union has honored its agreement completely.

What was the reaction of your professional staff?

The hardware and product design was all done in Milwaukee, in our industrial control group. Most of the software, however, had to be developed by our people down in Cleveland. Probably the most difficult thing to do in companies is to get divisions to cooperate with one another. Their priorities are all different, and we were taking resources away from each. People who were involved in the software development down in Cleveland saw this as an enormous technical challenge. I can assure you that people in Milwaukee don't think they got what they paid for. Engineers are all like that. And if you start a project with one engineer and then give it to another engineer, the new person wants to start over.

Also, our designers never had to work under the discipline this level of automation required. Everything had to be agreed on with the manufacturing engineers, everything had to be simulated, everything had to be executed within very tight rules. Designers started grumbling about the loss of their creativity. In the early days, there was a lot of bickering: "I can't design it because you tell me that you can't manufacture it! I'm going home." After a while, the designers came to the same conclusion we did—that if you didn't design under tight controls, the system wasn't going to work.

How did you get your suppliers to support such rigorous standards for quality?

We had intended to manufacture everything but coils, springs, screws, and little rubber doodads. Coils are not terribly challenging to control to the quality levels that we needed. But springs! There are all kinds of shapes and sizes of bloody little springs, and some of them go in holes half the size of my little finger. They don't hold tolerances very well. That whole project could have failed because of springs.

One of the guys we get springs from is fairly local—30, 40 miles away. He worked with us night and day, literally night and day. He got his process under control. We said, "There's going to be a lot of springs. When we get this thing running three shifts a day, five days a week, there's going to be one lot of springs. And if you think you can do it, we'll work with you. You're going to do one great amount of business with us." Bringing that supplier in as a partner was key.

How did you check him out?

In the past, we haven't worked with huge numbers of suppliers. We have extremely good engineers who can go out and look at the quality control processes they have, the equipment they have, their attitude. Generally, we want our suppliers to be roughly competitive, but we rarely sell at the lowest price, and we rarely buy at the lowest price either. Price is a criterion. I doubt seriously that those springs are at the lowest price that we could get. But they're suppose to go in those little holes, you see. We'd spend a lot more money if they wouldn't go in the holes.

Is it an inherent advantage for a company building CIM to be vertically integrated?

There are some components that have to be extraordinarily tightly controlled. You'd better control them yourself. In some cases, however, we ended up buying parts that we could have manufactured. One of our competitors in Germany had developed a very high-speed, highly automated contactor-tip manufacturing line. And our people came back and said, "How would you feel if we bought these machines from our competitor?" Well, I didn't care if we had bought them from Attila the Hun! So there are these four or five green machines in our factory with the name of our competitor. They sent us an engineer who stayed with us for more than a year.

The other area we didn't know anything about—nothing—was packaging. Keep in mind, each package had to be slightly different, each contactor has its own bar code—a lot size of one. We went with wonderful specifications and conceptual drawings up to this company in Minneapolis. And they said, "You must be nuts. Go away." We said, "No, no, no. You know how to do this. You're the best." We almost had to beg them. And so we've got slick packaging now. If we had tried to do that ourselves, we never would have made it.

You've worked closely with computer suppliers too, haven't you?

Yes, we have four different CAD systems in four locations. We have an IBM 3090 in Milwaukee, we have a Digital VAX system down in the factory, we have an Allen-Bradley Vista 2000 computer in the cell. We have several programmable-logic controllers in the cell. The real technological challenge has been getting all those computers working together.

This raises the question of software protocols. We see some movement toward common protocols, agreements hammered out between major computer companies and their clients. Do we need faster movement along these lines?

Well, the most progress is being made today in data communications, the MAP-TOP, or Manufacturing Automation Protocol and Technical Office Protocol. It's a single step, prompted by General Motors, toward making integration simple, more cost-effective, and more reliable. Remember, computer A speaks German, computer B speaks French, and computer D speaks Chinese. With MAP-TOP, we're not changing the fact that they do that; all we're doing is making them speak, say, English when they get on the network. They don't speak English any other time.

That's a tremendous step forward. But if we're aiming for the lowest cost and the highest performance, we have to have all of these computers on the same operating system—using the same protocols, the same syntax.

Are the leading computer companies doing their part to facilitate integration?

The big computer companies are eventually going to support a standard operating system, probably AT&T's UNIX. But IBM, Digital, Hewlett-Packard, God only knows who-all have now put $100 million into something out in California; they're going to have a different UNIX.

Now, you don't need two UNIX standards. If manufacturing companies like mine are going to say, okay, a standard operating system like UNIX forces us to make too many compromises on performance—

therefore, in certain applications, we're going to develop proprietary systems – that's fine. I think that's a very sensible thing to do. But why have two versions of UNIX? Why have two standard operating systems?

Won't the evolution of a standard operating system be particularly important to manufacturing?

I don't necessarily agree. In many cases, performance is more important.

Obviously, standardization of office communications protocols is overwhelmingly important. You wouldn't want two incompatible telephone systems. But manufacturing is very performance-driven. And though UNIX is a great operating system, it has a whole bunch of shortcomings. It feels like it was done by committee. Until the UNIX System V, it would have been described as a fragile operating system. I'm not technically proficient enough to explain why to you, but the Digital kind of operating system and the IBM system are very robust by comparison. I'll tell you, you don't mess around with UNIX. A few errors, it just dies.

> "If you can't understand the fundamentals of a technological decision, you're a figurehead. You're not the CEO."

You say you're no expert, but you seem to know a great deal more about these systems than most manufacturing executives. Wouldn't the standardization of operating systems, whatever the compromises on performance, help manufacturing executives who are technological novices?

Standardization would pave the way for more and more manufacturing software. There would be more vendors out there helping manufacturers get into projects they didn't think they could bring off. Still, I don't think we'd be well-advised to all move to one standard operating system right now. We'd lose too much performance, price performance as well.

Besides, if you're going to be a successful manager in a manufacturing company ten years from today, it will be mandatory for you to be technologically literate. You won't have to be an engineer. I've got a couple of young people at work for us who have some kind of arts degree. They're not rocket scientists. But they're very functional.

How did you become "functional"?

Five or six years ago, I'd never touched a computer. There's this huge gap between people who are over 40 and people who are under 20. Someday, the computer is going to feel like nothing more than a tool; that's not how it felt to me when I got started. I still think of computers in purely functional terms. Whether it has a 386 in it or it runs DOS, what the hell do I care? What I want to know is what it'll do for me. I'm not going to design one of these things, ever.

On the other hand, I probably learned twice as much as I should have because I got enamored with the technology. I also needed to understand enough to review a decision about spending $10 million. Should we develop a product with a UNIX operating system or should we do it with a proprietary operating system? Clearly, I need to know enough about the problem to make an intelligent decision.

You don't want to delegate a decision like that to somebody else.

No. If you can't understand the fundamentals of a decision, you're a figurehead. You're not the CEO.

What about people who've come up through the finance track or the marketing track? Is it conceivable that they could have had enough hands-on involvement with the technology to be effective leaders?

It hasn't been popular in most U.S. companies to make manufacturing a weapon. Manufacturers were thought of as people down in the black pit who threw things onto a truck. Strategy was thought to be all in product technology; the stars of the company were in the sales force.

We now have to elevate the importance of manufacturing. And I think that it's no good for people to come up from just one functional discipline and move in to run the company. I think you need to move people through the chairs and have them do a whole bunch of things before you tell them, "Go run this company." It's a brave new world. But you can't survive on bravery alone.

Reprint 89107

Must CIM be justified by faith alone?

"Managers need not – and should not – abandon the effort to justify computer-integrated manufacturing on financial grounds. Instead, they need ways to apply the DCF approach more appropriately."

Robert S. Kaplan

When the Yamazaki Machinery Company in Japan installed an $18 million flexible manufacturing system, the results were truly startling: a reduction in machines from 68 to 18, in employees from 215 to 12, in the floor space needed for production from 103,000 square feet to 30,000, and in average processing time from 35 days to 1.5.[1] After two years, however, total savings came to only $6.9 million, $3.9 million of which had flowed from a one-time cut in inventory. Even if the system continued to produce annual labor savings of $1.5 million for 20 years, the project's return would be less than 10% per year. Since many U.S. companies use hurdle rates of 15% or higher and payback periods of five years or less, they would find it hard to justify this investment in new technology – despite its enormous savings in number of employees, floor space, inventory, and throughput times.

The apparent inability of traditional modes of financial analysis like discounted cash flow to justify investments in computer-integrated manufacturing (CIM) has led a growing number of managers and observers to propose abandoning such criteria for CIM-related investments. "Let's be more practical," runs one such opinion. "DCF is not the only gospel. Many managers have become too absorbed with DCF to the extent that practical strategic directional considerations have been overlooked."[2]

Faced with outdated and inappropriate procedures of investment analysis, all that responsible executives can do is cast them aside in a bold leap of strategic faith. "Beyond all else," they have come to believe, "capital investment represents an act of faith, a belief that the future will be as promising as the present, together with a commitment to making the future happen."[3]

But must there be a fundamental conflict between the financial and the strategic justifications for CIM? It is unlikely that the theory of discounting future cash flow is either faulty or unimportant: receiving $1 in the future is worth less than receiving $1 today. If a company, even for good strategic reasons, consistently invests in projects whose financial returns are below its cost of capital, it will be on the road to insolvency. Whatever the special values of CIM technology, they cannot reverse the logic of the time value of money.

Surely, therefore, the trouble must not lie in some unbreachable gulf between the logic of DCF and the nature of CIM but in the poor application of DCF to these investment proposals. Managers need not – and should not – abandon the effort to justify CIM on financial grounds. Instead, they need ways to apply the DCF approach more appropriately and to be more sensitive to the realities and special attributes of CIM.

Mr. Kaplan is Arthur Lowes Dickinson Professor of Accounting at the Harvard Business School and a professor of industrial administration at Carnegie-Mellon University, where for six years he was dean of the business school. His first article for HBR, "Yesterday's Accounting Undermines Production" (July-August 1984), was a McKinsey Award winner.

Technical issues

The DCF approach most often goes wrong when companies set arbitrarily high hurdle rates for evaluating new investment projects. Perhaps they believe that high-return projects can be created by setting high rates rather than by making innovations in product and process technology or by cleverly building and exploiting a competitive advantage in the marketplace. In fact, the discounting function serves only to make cash flows received in the future equivalent to cash flows received now. For this narrow purpose—the only purpose, really, of discounting future cash flows—companies should use a discount rate based on the project's opportunity cost of capital (that is, the return available in the capital markets for investments of the same risk).

It may surprise managers to know that their real cost of capital can be in the neighborhood of 8%. (See Part I of the *Appendix* at the end of the article.) Double-digit hurdle rates that, in part, reflect assumptions of much higher capital costs are considerably wide of the mark. Their discouraging effect on CIM-type investments is not only unfortunate but also unfounded.

Companies also commonly underinvest in CIM and other new process technologies because they fail to evaluate properly all the relevant alternatives. Most of the capital expenditure requests I have seen measure new investments against a status quo alternative of making no new investments—an alternative that usually assumes a continuation of current market share, selling price, and costs. Experience shows, however, that the status quo rarely lasts. Business as usual does not continue undisturbed.

In fact, the correct alternative to new CIM investment should assume a situation of declining cash flows, market share, and profit margins. Once a valuable new process technology becomes available, even if one company decides not to invest in it, the likelihood is that some of its competitors will. As Henry Ford claimed, "If you need a new machine and don't buy it, you pay for it without getting it."[4] (For a more realistic approach to the evaluation of alternatives, see Part II of the *Appendix* at the end of the article.)

A related problem with current practice is its bias toward incremental rather than revolutionary projects. In many companies, the capital approval process specifies different levels of authorization depending on the size of the request. Small investments (under $100,000, say) may need only the approval of the plant manager; expenditures in excess of several million dollars may require the board of directors' approval. This apparently sensible procedure, however, creates an incentive for managers to propose small projects that fall just below the cut-off point where higher level approval would be needed. Over time, a host of little investments, each of which delivers savings in labor, material, or overhead cost, can add up to a less-than-optimal pattern of material flow and to obsolete process technology. (Part III of the *Appendix* shows the consequences of this incremental bias in more detail.)

"I still think 'Buyout' is not a proper name for a dog."

Introducing CIM process technology is not, of course, without its costs. Out-of-pocket equipment expense is only the beginning. Less obvious are the associated software costs that are necessary for CIM equipment to operate effectively. Managers should not be misled by the expensing of these costs for tax and financial reporting purposes into thinking them operating expenses rather than investments. For internal management purposes, software development is as much a part of the investment in CIM equipment as the physical hardware itself. Indeed, in some installations, the programming, debugging, and prototype development may cost more than the hardware.

There are still other initial costs: site preparation, conveyors, transfer devices, feeders, parts orientation, and spare parts for the CIM equipment. Operating and maintenance personnel must be retrained and new operating procedures developed. Like software development, these tax-deductible training and education costs are part of the investment in CIM, not an expense of the periods in which they happen to be incurred.

Further, as some current research has shown, noteworthy declines in productivity often accompany the introduction of new process technology.[5] These productivity declines can last up to a year, even longer when a radical new technology like CIM is installed. Apparently, the new equipment introduces severe and unanticipated process disruptions, which lead to equipment breakdowns that are higher than expected; to operating, repair, and maintenance problems; to scheduling and coordination difficulties; to revised materials standards; and to old-fashioned confusion on the factory floor.

We do not yet know how much of the disruption is caused by inadequate planning. After investing considerable effort and anguish in the equipment acquisition decision, some companies no doubt revert to business as usual while waiting for the new equipment to arrive.

Whatever the cause, the productivity decline is particularly ill timed since it occurs just when a company is likely to conduct a postaudit on whether it is realizing the anticipated savings from the new equipment. Far from achieving anticipated savings, the postaudit will undoubtedly reveal lower output and higher costs than predicted.

Tangible benefits

The usual difficulties in carrying out DCF analysis—choosing an appropriate discount rate and evaluating correctly all relevant investment alternatives—apply with special force to the consideration of investments in CIM process technology. The greater flexibility of CIM technology, which allows it to be used for successive generations of products, gives it a longer useful life than traditional process investments. Because its benefits are likely to persist longer, overestimating the relevant discount rate will penalize CIM investments disproportionately more than shorter lived investments. The compounding effect of excessively high annual interest rates causes future cash flows to be discounted much too severely. Further, if executives arbitrarily specify short payback periods for new investments, the effect will be to curtail more CIM investments than traditional bottleneck-relief projects.

But beyond a longer useful life, CIM technology provides many additional benefits—better quality, greater flexibility, reduced inventory and floor space, lower throughput times, experience with new technology—that a typical capital justification process does not quantify. Financial analyses that focus too narrowly on easily quantified savings in labor, materials, or energy will miss important benefits from CIM technology.

Inventory savings

Some of these omissions can be easily remedied. The process flexibility, more orderly product flow, higher quality, and better scheduling that are typical of properly used CIM equipment will drastically cut both work-in-process (WIP) and finished goods inventory levels. This reduction in average inventory levels represents a large cash inflow at the time the new process equipment becomes operational. This, of course, is a cash savings that DCF analysis can easily capture.

Consider a product line for which the anticipated monthly cost of sales is $500,000. Using existing equipment and technology, the producing division carries about three months of sales in inventory. After investing in flexible automation, the division heads find that reduced waste, scrap, and rework, greater predictability, and faster throughput permit a two-thirds reduction in average inventory levels. (This is not an unrealistic assumption: Murata Machinery Ltd. has reported that its FMS installation permitted a two-thirds reduction in workers, a 450% increase in output, and a 75% cut in inventory levels.[6])

Pruning inventory from three months to one month of sales produces a cash inflow of $1 million in the first year the system becomes operational. If sales increase 10% per year, the company will enjoy increased cash flows from the inventory reductions in all future years too—that is, if the cost of sales rises to $550,000 in the next year, a two-month reduction

Example of an FMS justification analysis

With the following analysis, one U.S. manufacturer of air-handling equipment justified its investment in an FMS installation for producing a key component:

1
Internal manufacture of the component is essential for the division's long-term strategy to maintain its capability to design and manufacture a proprietary product.

2
The component has been manufactured on mostly conventional equipment—some numerically controlled—with an average age of 23 years. To manufacture a product in conformance with current quality specifications, the company must replace this equipment with new conventional equipment or advanced technology.

3
The alternatives are:
Conventional or numerically controlled stand-alone.
Transfer line.
Machining cells.
FMS.

4
FMS compares with conventional technology as Table A shows.

5
Intangible benefits include virtually unlimited flexibility for FMS to modify mix of component models to the exact requirements of the assembly department.

6
The financial analysis for a project life of ten years compares the FMS with conventional technology (static sales assumptions, constant, or base-year, dollars) as Table B shows.

7
With dynamic sales assumptions showing expected increases in production volume, the annual operating savings will double in future years and the financial yield (still using constant, base-year, dollars) will increase to more than 17% per year.

On the basis of this analysis and recognizing the value of the intangible item (5), which had not been incorporated formally, the company selected the FMS option.

Table A

	Conventional equipment	FMS
Utilization	30%-40%	80%-90%
Number of employees needed (including indirect workers, such as those who do materials handling, inspection, and rework)*	52	14
Reduced scrap and rework	–	$60,000 annually
Inventory	$2,000,000	$1,100,000†
Incremental investment	–	$9,200,000

*Each employee costs $36,000 a year in wages and fringe benefits.
†Inventory reductions because of shorter lead times and flexibility.

Table B

Year	Investment	Operating savings	Tax savings ITC and ACRS depreciation	After-tax cash flow 50%
0	$9,200	$ 900‡	$ 920	$ −7,380
1		1,428§	1,311	1,370¶
2		1,428	1,923	1,675
3		1,428	1,835	1,632
4		1,428	1,835	1,632
5		1,428	1,835	1,632
6		1,428		714
7		1,428		714
8		1,428		714
9		1,428		714
10		1,428		714

After-tax yield: 11.1%.
Payback period: during year 5.

‡$ 900 = Inventory reduction at start of project.

§$ 1,428 = 38 fewer employees at $36,000/year + $60,000 scrap and rework savings.

¶$ 1,370 = (1,428) (1 − 0.50) + (1,311) (0.50).

in inventory saves an additional $100,000 that year, $110,000 the year after, and $121,000 the year after that.

Less floor space

CIM also cuts floor-space requirements. It takes fewer computer-controlled machines to do the same job as a larger number of conventional machines. Also, the factory floor will no longer be used to store inventory. Recall the example of the Japanese plant that installed a flexible manufacturing system and reduced space requirements from 103,000 to 30,000 square feet. These space savings are real, but conventional financial accounting systems do not measure their value well—especially if the building is almost fully depreciated or was purchased years before when price levels were lower. Do not, therefore, look to financial accounting systems for a good estimate of the cost or value of space. Instead, compute the estimate in terms of the opportunity cost of new space: either its square-foot rental value or the annualized cost of new construction.

Many companies that have installed CIM technology have discovered a new factory inside their old one. This new "factory within a factory" occupies the space where excessive WIP inventory and infrequently used special-purpose machines used to sit. Eliminating WIP inventory and rationalizing machine layout can easily lead to savings of more than 50% in floor space. In practice, these savings have enabled some companies to curtail plant and office expansion programs and, on occasion, to fold the operations of a second factory (which could then be sold off at current market prices) into the reorganized original factory.

Higher quality

Greatly improved quality, defined here as conformance to specifications, is a third tangible benefit from investment in CIM technology. Automated process equipment leads directly to more uniform production and, frequently, to an order-of-magnitude decline in defects. These benefits are easy to quantify and should be part of any cash flow analysis. Some managers have seen five- to tenfold reductions in waste, scrap, and rework when they replaced manual operations with automated equipment.

Further, as production uniformity increases, fewer inspection stations and fewer inspectors are required. If automatic gauging is included in the CIM installation, virtually all manual inspection of parts can be eliminated. Also, with 100% continuous automated inspection, out-of-tolerance parts are detected immediately. With manual systems, the entire lot of parts to be produced before a problem is detected would need to be reworked or scrapped.

These capabilities lead, in turn, to significant reductions in warranty expense. When General Electric automated its dishwasher operation, for example, its service call rate fell 50%. Designing manufacturability into products, making the production process more reliable and uniform, and improving automated inspection can all contribute to major cash flow savings. Although it may be hard to estimate these savings out to four or five significant digits, it would be grossly wrong to assume that the benefits are zero. We must overcome the preference of accountants for precision over accuracy, which causes them to ignore benefits they cannot quantify beyond one or two digits of accuracy.

We can estimate still other tangible benefits from CIM. John Shewchuk of General Electric claims that accounts receivable can be reduced by eliminating the incidence of customers who defer payment until quality problems are resolved.[7] Consider too that because improved materials flow can reduce the need for forklift trucks and operators, factories will enjoy a large cash flow saving from not having to acquire, maintain, repair, and operate so many trucks. All these calculations belong in a company's capital justification process.

Intangible benefits

Other benefits of CIM include increased flexibility, faster response to market shifts, and greatly reduced throughput and lead times. These benefits are as important as those just discussed but much harder to quantify. We may not be sure how many zeros should be in our benefits estimate (are they to be measured in thousands or millions of dollars?) much less which digit should be first. The difficulty arises in large part because these benefits represent revenue enhancements rather than cost savings. It is fairly easy to get a ballpark estimate for percentage reductions in costs already being incurred. It is much harder to quantify the magnitude of revenue enhancement expected from features that are not already in place.

Greater flexibility

The flexibility that CIM technology offers takes several forms. The benefits of economies of scope—that is, the potential for low-cost production of high-variety, low-volume goods – are just beginning to flow from FMS environments as early adopters of the technology start to service after-market sales for discontinued models on the same equipment used to produce current high-volume models. We are also beginning to see some customized production on the same lines used for standard products.

Beyond these economy-of-scope applications, CIM's reprogramming capabilities make it possible for machines to serve as backups for each other. Even if a machine is dedicated to a narrow product line, it can still replace lost production during a second or a third shift when a similar piece of equipment, producing quite a different product, breaks down.

Further, by easily accommodating engineering change orders and product redesigns, CIM technology allows for product changes over time. And, if the mix of products demanded by the market changes, a CIM-based process can respond with no increase in costs. The body shop of one automobile assembly plant, for example, quickly adjusted its flexible, programmed spot-welding robots to a shift in consumer preference from the two-door to the four-door version of a certain car model. Had the line been equipped with nonprogrammable welding equipment, the adjustment would have been far more costly.

CIM's flexibility also gives it usefulness beyond the life cycle of the product for which it was purchased. True, in the short run, CIM may perform the same functions as less expensive, inflexible equipment. Many benefits of its flexibility will show up only over time. Therefore, it is difficult to estimate how much this flexibility will be worth. Nonetheless, as we shall see, even an order-of-magnitude estimate may be sufficient.

Shorter throughput & lead time

Another seemingly intangible benefit of CIM is the great reductions it makes possible in throughput and lead time. At the Yamazaki factory described at the beginning of this article, average processing time per work piece fell from 35 to 1.5 days. Other installations, including Yamazaki's Mazak plant in Florence, Kentucky, have reported similar savings, ranging from a low of 50% reduction in processing time to a maximum of nearly 95%. To be sure, some of the benefits from greatly reduced throughput times have already been incorporated in our estimate of savings from inventory reductions. But there is also a notable marketing advantage in being able to meet customer demands with shorter lead times and to respond quickly to changes in market demand.

Increased learning

Some investments in new process technology have important learning characteristics. Thus, even if calculations of the net present value of their cash flows turn up negative, the investments can still be quite valuable by permitting managers to gain experience with the technology, test the market for new products, and keep a close watch on major process advances.

These learning effects have characteristics similar to buying options in financial markets. Buying options may not at first seem like a favorable investment, but quite small initial outlays may yield huge benefits down the line. Similarly, were a company to invest in a risky CIM-related project, it could reap big gains should the technology provide unexpected competitive advantages in the future. Moreover, given the rapid pace of technological change and the advantages of being an early market participant, companies that defer process investments until the new technology is well established will find themselves far behind the market leaders. In this context, the decision to defer investment is often a decision not to be a principal player in the next round of product or process innovation.

The companies that in the mid-1970s invested in automatic and electronically controlled machine tools were well positioned to exploit the microprocessor-based revolution in capabilities – much higher performance at much lower cost – that hit during the early 1980s. Because operators, maintenance personnel, and process engineers were already comfortable with electronic technology, it was relatively simple to retrofit existing machines with powerful microelectronics. Companies that had earlier deferred investment in electronically controlled machine tools fell behind: they had acquired no option on these new process technologies.

The bottom line

Although intangible benefits may be difficult to quantify, there is no reason to value them at zero in a capital expenditure analysis. Zero is, after all, no less arbitrary than any other number. Conservative accountants who assign zero values to many intangible benefits prefer being precisely wrong to being vaguely right. Managers need not follow their example.

Author's note: Especially helpful comments on the preliminary draft were made by Robin Cooper and Robert Hayes (Harvard Business School), Alan Kantrow (*Harvard Business Review*), George Kuper (Manufacturing Studies Board), and Scott Richard and Jeff Williams (Carnegie-Mellon).

One way to combine difficult-to-measure benefits with those more easily quantified is, first, to estimate the annual cash flows about which there is the greatest confidence: the cost of the new process equipment and the benefits expected from labor, inventory, floor space, and cost-of-quality savings. If at this point a discounted cash flow analysis–done with a sensible discount rate and a consideration of all relevant alternatives–shows a CIM investment to have a positive net present value, well and good. Even without accounting for the value of intangible benefits, the analysis will have gotten the project over its financial hurdle. If the DCF is negative, however, then it becomes necessary to estimate how much the annual cash flows must increase before the investment does have a positive net present value.

Suppose, for example, that an extra $100,000 per year over the life of the investment is sufficient to give the project the desired return. Then management can decide whether it expects heightened flexibility, reduced throughput and lead times, and faster market response to be worth at least $100,000 per year. Should the company be willing to pay $100,000 annually to enjoy these benefits? If so, it can accept the project with confidence. If, however, the additional cash flows needed to justify the investment turn out to be quite large–say $3 million per year–and management decides the intangible benefits of CIM are not worth that sum, then it is perfectly sensible to turn the investment down.

Rather than attempt to put a dollar tag on benefits that by their nature are difficult to quantify, managers should reverse the process and estimate first how large these benefits must be in order to justify the proposed investment. Senior executives can be expected to judge that improved flexibility, rapid customer service, market adaptability, and options on new process technology may be worth $300,000 to $500,000 per year but not, say, $1 million. This may not be exact mathematics, but it does help put a meaningful price on CIM's intangible benefits.

As manufacturers make critical decisions about whether to acquire CIM equipment, they must avoid claims that such investments have to be made on faith alone because financial analysis is too limiting. Successful process investments must yield returns in excess of the cost of capital invested. That is only common sense. Thus the challenge for managers is to improve their ability to estimate the costs and benefits of CIM, not to take the easy way out and discard the necessary discipline of financial analysis.

References

1 This example has appeared in several articles on strategic justification for flexible automation projects. Clifford Young of Arthur D. Little has traced the example to *American Market/Metalworking News*, October 26, 1981. Other examples of the labor, machinery, and throughput savings from flexible manufacturing system installations are presented in Anderson Ashburn and Joseph Jablonowski, "Japan's Builders Embrace FMS," *American Machinist*, February 1985, p. 83.

2 John P. Van Blois, "Economic Models: The Future of Robotic Justification," Thirteenth ISIR/Robots 7 Conference, April 17-21, 1983 (available from Society of Manufacturing Engineers, Dearborn, Michigan).

3 Robert H. Hayes and David A. Garvin, "Managing As If Tomorrow Mattered," HBR May-June 1982, p. 70.

4 Quoted in John Shewchuk, "Justifying Flexible Automation," *American Machinist*, October 1984, p. 93.

5 See Robert H. Hayes and Kim B. Clark, "Exploring the Sources of Productivity Differences at the Factory Level," in *The Uneasy Alliance: Managing the Productivity-Technology Dilemma*, ed. Kim B. Clark, Robert H. Hayes, and Christopher Lorenz (Boston: Harvard Business School Press, 1985), and Bruce Chew, "Productivity and Change: Understanding Productivity at the Factory Level," Harvard Business School Working Paper (1985).

6 "Japan's Builders Embrace FMS," *American Machinist*, February 1985, p. 83.

7 John Shewchuk, "Justifying Flexible Automation."

[See the Appendix on page 78.]

Appendix

Getting the numbers right

Part I
The cost of capital

A company always has the option of repurchasing its common shares or retiring its debt. Therefore, managers can estimate the cost of capital for a project by taking a weighted average of the current cost of equity and debt at the mix of capital financing typical in the industry. Extensive studies of the returns to investors in equity and fixed-income markets during the past 60 years show that from 1926 to 1984 the average total return (dividends plus price appreciation) from holding a diversified portfolio of common stocks was 11.7% per year. This return already includes the effects of rising price levels. Removing the effects of inflation puts the real (after-inflation) return from investments in common stocks at about 8.5% per year (see Table A).*

These historical estimates of 8.5% real (or about 12% nominal) are, however, overestimates of the total cost of capital. From 1926 to 1984, fixed-income securities averaged nominal before-tax returns of less than 5% per year. Taking out inflation reduces the real return (or cost) of high-grade corporate debt securities to about 1.5% per year. Even with recent increases in the real interest rate, a mixture of debt and equity financing produces a total real cost of capital of less than 8%.

Many corporate executives will, no doubt, be highly skeptical that their real cost of capital could be 8% or less. Their disbelief probably comes from making one of two conceptual errors, perhaps both. First, executives often attempt to estimate their current cost of capital by looking at their accounting return on investment – that is, the net income divided by the net invested capital – of their divisions or corporations. For many companies this figure can be in the 15% to 25% range.

There are several reasons, however, why an accounting ROI is a poor estimate of a company's real cost of capital. The accounting ROI figure is distorted by financial accounting conventions such as depreciation method and a variety of capitalization and expense decisions. The ROI figure is also distorted by management's failure to adjust both the net income and the invested capital figures for the effects of inflation, an omission that biases the accounting ROI well above the company's actual real return on investment.

The second conceptual error that makes an 8% real cost of capital sound too low is implicitly to compare it with today's market interest rates and returns on common stocks. These rates incorporate expectations of current and future inflation, but the 8.5% historical return on common stocks and the less than 2% return on fixed-income securities are *real* returns, after the effects of inflation have been netted out.

Now it is possible, of course, to do a DCF analysis by using nominal market returns as a way of estimating a company's cost of capital. In fact, this may even be desirable when you are doing an after-tax cash flow analysis since one of the important cash flows being discounted is the nominal tax depreciation shield from new investments. I have, however, seen many a company go seriously wrong by using a nominal discount rate (say in excess of 15%) while it was assuming level cash flows over the life of their investments.

Consider, for example, the data in Table B, which is excerpted from an actual capital authorization request. Notice that all the cash flows during the ten years of the project's expected life are expressed in 1977 dollars, even though the company used a 20% discount rate on the cash flows of the several investment alternatives. This assumption of a 20% cost of capital most likely arose from a prior assumption of a real cost of capital of about 10% and an expected inflation rate of 10% per year. But if it believed that inflation would average 10% annually over the life of the project, the company should also have raised the assumed selling price and the unit costs of labor, material, and overhead by their expected price increases over the life of the project.

It is inconsistent to assume a high rate of inflation for the interest rate used in a DCF calculation but a zero rate of price change when you are estimating future net cash flows from an investment. Naturally, this inconsistency – using double-digit discount rates but level cash flows – biases the analysis toward the rejection of new investments, especially those yielding benefits five to ten years into the future. Compounding excessively high interest rates will place a low value on cash flows in these later years: a 20% interest rate, for example, discounts $1.00 to $.40 in five years and to $.16 in ten years. If companies use discount rates derived from current market rates of return, then they must also estimate rates of price and cost changes for all future cash flows.

Table A   **Annual return series**
1926-1984

Mean annual returns

Series	1926-1984	1950-1984	1975-1984
Common stocks	11.7 %	12.8 %	14.7 %
Long-term corporate bonds	4.7	4.5	8.4
U.S. Treasury bills	3.4	5.1	9.0
Inflation (CPI)	3.2	4.4	7.4

Real annual returns
net of inflation

Series	1926-1984	1950-1984	1975-1984
Common stocks	8.5 %	8.4 %	7.3 %
Long-term corporate bonds	1.5	0.1	1.0
U.S. Treasury bills	0.2	0.6	1.6

Must CIM be justified by faith alone? 79

Part II
Measuring alternatives

Look again at the capital authorization request in *Table B*. The cash flows from alternative 1 assume a constant level of sales during the next ten years; the cash flows from alternative 5 show a somewhat higher level of sales based on a small increase in market share. The difference in sales revenue as currently projected, however, is not all that great. Only if managers anticipate a steady decrease in market share and sales revenue for alternative 1, a decrease occasioned by domestic or international competitors adopting the new production technology, would alternative 5 show a major improvement over the status quo.

Obviously, not all investments in new process technology are investments that should be made. Even if competitors adopt new technology and profits erode over time, a company may still find that the benefits from investing would not compensate for its costs. But either way, the company should rest its decision on a correct reading of what is likely to happen to cash flows when it rejects a new technology investment.

Table B **Example of a capital authorization request***

Alternative 1	Rebuild present machines						
Year	1977	1978	1979	1980	1981	...	1986
Sales	$ 6,404	$ 6,404	$ 6,404	$ 6,404	$ 6,404	...	$ 6,404
Cost of sales:							
Labor	168	168	168	168	168	...	168
Material	312	312	312	312	312	...	312
Overhead	1,557	1,557	1,557	1,557	1,557	...	1,557
Alternative 5	**Purchase all new machines**						
Year	1977	1978	1979	1980	1981	...	1986
Sales	$ 6,404	$ 6,724	$ 7,060	$ 7,413	$ 7,784	...	$ 7,784
Cost of sales:							
Labor	167	154	148	152	152	...	152
Material	312	328	344	361	380	...	380
Overhead	1,557	1,440	1,390	1,423	1,423	...	1,423

*Adapted from Robert S. Kaplan and Glen Bingham, *Wilmington Tap and Die*, Case 185-124 (Boston: Harvard Business School, 1985).

Part III
Piecemeal investment

Each year, a company or a division may undertake a series of small improvements in its production process—to alleviate bottlenecks, to add capacity where needed, or to introduce islands of automation based on immediate and easily quantified labor savings. Each of these projects, taken by itself, may have a positive net present value. By investing on a piecemeal basis, however, the company or division will never get the full benefit of completely redesigning and rebuilding its plant. Yet the pressures to go forward on a piecemeal basis are nearly irresistible. At any point in time, there are many annual, incremental projects scattered about from which the investment has yet to be recovered. Thus, were management to scrap the plant, its past incremental investments would be shown to be incorrect.

One alternative to this piecemeal approach is to forecast the remaining technological life of the plant and then to enforce a policy of accepting no process improvements that will not be repaid within this period. Managers can treat the money that otherwise would have been invested as if it accrued interest at the company's cost of capital. At the end of the specified period, they could abandon the old facility and build a new one with the latest relevant technology.

Although none of the usual incremental process investments may have been incorrect, the collection of incremental decisions could have a lower net present value than the alternative of deferring most investment during a terminal period, earning interest on the unexpended funds, and then replacing the plant. Again, the failure to evaluate such global investment is not a limitation of DCF analysis. It is a failure of not applying DCF analysis to all the feasible alternatives to annual, incremental investment proposals.

---

*Roger G. Ibbotson and Rex A. Sinquefield, *Stocks, Bonds, Bills and Inflation: The Past and the Future* (Charlottesville, Va.: Financial Analysts Research Foundation, 1982). The author has updated this study for returns earned during 1982-1984.

This estimate should be adjusted up or down, depending on whether the project's risk is above or below the risk of the average project in the market. A detailed discussion of appropriate risk adjustments is beyond the scope of this article. Good treatments can be found in David W. Mullins, Jr., "Does the Capital Asset Pricing Model Work?" HBR January-February 1982, p. 105, and in chap. 7-9 in Richard Brealey and Stewart Myers, *Principles of Corporate Finance*, 2d ed. (New York: McGraw-Hill, 1984).

Information and the Organization

SPECIAL REPORT

How to centralize the information systems function without losing responsiveness to technology users

The 'Centrally Decentralized' IS Organization

by Ernest M. von Simson

The death of the corporate mainframe has been greatly exaggerated. After a period in which many companies experimented with decentralizing their information systems (IS) organization, the pendulum is swinging back once again. Companies are consolidating data centers, beefing up the authority of their central IS staffs, and establishing companywide technical standards and work procedures.

There are three factors driving this trend toward recentralization:

1. The high cost of multiple data-processing facilities – in particular, the costs of licensing software at many different sites. Companies can no longer ignore the cost-effectiveness of consolidation. For most, just two mainframe centers provide sufficient redundancy of operations.

2. The changing demographics of the information systems profession. Demand is growing just as supply is declining. Creating clear career paths in a central IS staff offers the professional opportunities likely to attract high-quality people.

3. The emphasis on companywide information systems that integrate business functions and support new business opportunities. A central IS staff with a broad overview of the company's information needs can champion integration far more effectively than decentralized IS units. This is the real strategic payoff of centralization.

But recentralization does *not* mean a return to the entrenched and unresponsive IS bureaucracies of the past. Instead, a hybrid organizational model is emerging, one that promises to transcend the traditional trade-off between centralization and decentralization once and for all.

If a solid line symbolizes reporting relationships in the traditional centralized IS organization and a dotted line those of the decentralized alternative, then this new model requires what might be called "striped-line" reporting, with genuine power sharing between IS managers and users. A central IS organization is responsible for the company's technological infrastructure and for selecting and training technical staff. But the development of new computer applications is handled in a decentralized fashion, following priorities and budgets set by the users.

At one multinational corporation, for example, business unit IS managers and staffs belong to the central IS organization, which handles recruiting, training, and promotion ladders. Staff size and budget decisions, however, are negotiated between business unit heads and the COO. Information systems executives neither attend the meetings where such matters are discussed nor defend the business unit budget for information systems. Steering committees within the business units set priorities for new applications. Local IS managers participate – but only as nonvoting recording secretaries. Performance appraisals for IS staff are the joint responsibility of business unit heads and the central IS executive, with more weight given to the views of the line department.

Hybrid IS organizations like this one are a response to the shortcomings of previous organizational models. In the early days of corporate computing, companies centralized the IS function to promote cost efficiencies and greater professionalism – but at the price of a bureaucracy prone to stagnation, too remote from business pressures and strategies, and unresponsive to user needs. Decentralization, where each business unit or function has its own IS department and creates its own systems, was an attempt to solve that

---

Ernest M. von Simson is a senior partner at the Research Board, a New York-based private research organization sponsored by 80 large corporations that are major users of information technology. Over the last decade, he has helped write some 60 case studies describing the present shape and future direction of corporate information systems organizations.

problem. It minimized turf battles over budget allocations and ensured closer connections to users – but too often with the result of creating a rudderless IS staff. A striped-line IS organization delivers the best of both worlds – the cost savings and control of centralization with the user-responsiveness and flexibility of decentralization.

This conclusion is the product of a confidential study I conducted with colleagues at the Research Board. We toured 30 member companies – 10 in manufacturing, 10 in finance, and another 10 selected from the transportation, retail, and engineering-contracting sectors. We interviewed IS senior executives in all these organizations as well as some CEOs and corporate users.

All of the companies we studied are large. The smallest has about $2 billion in annual revenues and fully half have over $10 billion. The Research Board has also extensively studied more than half of these companies in the past, which gives us a unique longitudinal perspective on the lessons learned.

The reemergence of the mainframe

The advantages of centralization are clearest in computer operations – the mainframes, networks, and data-processing and storage facilities that make up a company's technological infrastructure.

The primary incentive for consolidating computer operations is higher site-licensing fees for systems software. Traditionally, computer vendors have chosen to keep their hardware prices competitive and profit from the licensing of their proprietary software. Companies pay for databases and operating systems by the number of copies they need. Thus the more data centers, the higher the software costs. The smartest companies are responding to this vendor practice by consigning the essential software to fewer locations, resulting in lower licensing expenditures. Of necessity, those central sites are much larger than the more dispersed centers of the past.

The potential cost savings from centralization are causing even those companies deeply committed to business unit independence to consolidate data centers. Consider the example of one consumer products company we studied, whose superb growth is based on acquiring independent brands and nurturing their distinct images. Despite this decentralized corporate structure, the CEO decided to consolidate all computer facilities into two centrally managed centers when planners told him this

> **Centralization can cut a computer-operations budget by up to 20%.**

would save about $3 million per year. The actual savings turned out to be nearly three times as large. At least 20% of the company's $40 million annual computer-operations budget has been eliminated – simply by cross-utilizing technical staff and reducing software licenses.

Other companies are making similar decisions. In our sample, 17 had recently reorganized their computer operations at the time we visited them. All but one had moved in the direction of increased centralization, consolidating many small data centers into a few large ones. (Of the remaining 13 companies, 8 had never experimented with decentralization; 2 used dispersed facilities but still managed them centrally through the corporate IS staff; and only 3 gave decentralized management responsibility to business units or departments.)

At one large financial institution that processes credit card transactions, consolidation has produced equipment efficiencies, head-count reductions, and other cost savings. Unit costs per transaction have dropped 25% annually since consolidation. Systems availability, the amount of time computers are actually processing, has improved from 95% to over 99.5%. And telecommunications costs have declined $6 million per year. When the company took over processing for a new credit card, the customer's annual computing bill dropped by $4 million.

The decline in long-distance communications rates has contributed to consolidation. As the cost of communicating with mainframes at a remote site drops, it becomes less necessary to have multiple data centers near local business offices. The greatest advantages of consolidation accrue to those companies with the technical know-how to buy transmission services in bulk and use sophisticated equipment for networking between factories and offices and data centers. One company in our sample realized a 35% annual return on its telecommunications and infrastructure investments – while doubling its communications capacity.

Centralizing data centers also lets a company take advantage of unexpected opportunities for volume discounts, special terms, extra support, and other concessions from technology suppliers. Contract specialists on the central IS staff can negotiate and administer nationwide and worldwide agreements. For example, one petroleum company has achieved increased leverage with its computer suppliers and third-party lessors, thanks to an aggressive central contracting unit staffed with knowledgeable negotiators. Its volume contracts reflect the IS department's worldwide clout – something that would be unavailable to any divisional purchasing agent.

Finally, centralized operations are more likely to use the newest productivity tools for data processing. In general, the bigger the center, the better the quality of management and the more adept it is at using such tools. What's more, the cost of implementing these tools is lower in one or two centers than in many.

Even when companies don't go all the way in consolidating data centers, they are centralizing employees who have software expertise – for mainframes, minis, and in some cases even personal computers. At a global chemical giant with an inviolate tradition of business unit autonomy, a central IS staff supports 300 minicomputer sites around the world. Technicians at headquarters troubleshoot software from three computer vendors over telephone lines. This spares business unit managers the effort of recruiting, training, and supervising their own technical experts. And the company gets competence, efficiency, and a far more consistent technological infrastructure than one would expect, given the organization's decentralized corporate culture.

Attracting first-rate IS professionals

Another factor pushing companies to recentralize is the looming shortage of qualified IS personnel. The pool of computer-science degree graduates is actually declining, and companies increasingly find themselves competing with the growing number of computer software and service entrepreneurs for qualified staff. As a result, salaries are skyrocketing, and entry-level staff people are no longer willing to take any journeyman job in information systems.

The need to attract and retain a professional IS staff is encouraging some centralization even where the logic of decentralization is strongest: applications development. Although many experts assumed that more powerful and user-friendly microcomputers would liberate users from the need for centralized technical expertise, the reality is just the opposite. The typical PC user's image of total self-sufficiency quickly wilts when faced with sophisticated graphics, complex networks, incompatible architectures, alternative databases, or a Babel of languages and interfaces.

To get quality employees who can provide this expertise, companies need to offer them an attractive career path—especially for highly paid mid-career professionals. A central staff at corporate headquarters with a solid promotion ladder within the discipline is a credible platform for career advancement; a vague hope of "general business" opportunities is not. Companies that cannot offer clear opportunities for career development are likely to find they cannot attract and retain the best people.

Centralizing the IS staff has other advantages. For instance, the quality and cost per student hour of training and retraining improves when training is centrally coordinated and monitored. And centralization also makes possible career movement across divisions, which serves to broaden the individual's expertise and counteract the complacency likely to develop in isolated IS units.

At a global chemical company, the central IS department handles all entry-level hiring and training for systems specialists. Every new crop of college recruits first completes a series of formal courses on productivity tools and applications-development standards used throughout the corporation, then moves through an entry-level tour in various business units. After three years, successful apprentices choose

> **The key force driving recentralization: the growing reliance on integrated systems.**

longer term IS assignments anywhere they wish in the company—taking along with them a consistent approach to applications development as well as working relationships with counterparts throughout the organization.

In a diversified financial institution, consistent appraisal practices now apply across all IS groups. IS executives fill open supervisory positions from a list of the three most deserving IS candidates in the entire corporation, not just in the unit in question. This allows the IS organization to provide its employees with experience in many different parts of the company (which encourages integration), while building their loyalty to the IS department. Business unit managers like the approach as well because they have a much broader choice among staff than simply the next IS person in line in their unit. Likewise, downsizing efforts focus on the worst performers *anywhere* in the company—so recently recruited staff aren't automatically lost to the company just because one business unit suffers a down-draft. Instead, better performers are reassigned to other segments of the corporation.

The rise of integrated systems

Probably the most important force driving the trend toward recentralization is the growing reliance on integrated systems. No matter what the business, getting to market faster requires closer links among design, production, and service activities. And taking advantage of new business opportunities means extending integration beyond the company itself to include deep, direct information exchanges with customers and suppliers. Information technology is the glue of these integrated business activities.

At the companies we studied, integration is taking many forms:

☐ One diverse industrial company created a new customer services unit to give its biggest customers a single contact point, covering everything from order entry to accounts receivable. A single representative now handles shipment tracking, technical questions, billings, and other service activities for the customer. The logic is to make the *process* of doing business with the company a *reason* to do business with it. But unified service required territorial sacrifices from the marketing, finance, and research departments, as well as integration of their once-separate computer systems into a common front end.

☐ An insurance company is applying the "quick response" objectives of modern manufacturing to its operations—from order entry to product shipment. Until recently, applications for new policies had to cross 20 separate desks—some of them several times—and an unknown number of computer systems. This cumbersome process created an "information float" that consumed 25 days in the 26-day policy-issuing cycle. Streamlining this process meant redefining department objectives, breaking down the boundaries between functions, and designing systems that facilitate organizational integration.

☐ In a highly decentralized company, where the product lines range from aerospace to electronics to automotive parts, each business unit reaches entirely different markets, uses different base technologies, and pursues different product-introduction rates. But they share a new corporate-purchasing database encompassing all the thousands of vendors used throughout the company. This allows each business unit to negotiate prices and terms with suppliers on the strength of the entire corporate relationship. Creating that database required coordinated feeds from the purchasing systems of each independent business unit and company-wide agreement on consolidating 100,000 vendor account numbers.

☐ Several consumer products companies have also established umbrella sales organizations over their previously autonomous product divisions—but only after major retailers demanded an end to visits from multiple sales representatives. Likewise, a foreign bank is creating a successful mortgage business by using its real estate subsidiary's database for "intramural" referrals.

None of these systems would have been possible without a strong, central IS staff with a strategic overview of the business. A centralized IS department can see beyond the sometimes parochial objectives of different departments or business units and break up bureaucratic information flows to take advantage of new business opportunities.

The best of both worlds

Obituaries for the glass house where mainframes reside were obviously premature. But recentralization won't save central IS groups that ignore the importance of responsiveness to users or refuse to break the rigidly technocratic shell that fostered IS fragmentation in the first place. By now, many IS executives understand this perfectly well. That's why they are defining a hybrid model that allows companies to exploit the advantages of centralization without losing the flexibility of decentralization.

In this model, corporate IS operates the consolidated computing and communications network; takes responsibility for staff recruitment, training, and management rotation; establishes the technological "spinal cord"; and sets standards for databases, programming tools, and the design of applications. Meanwhile,

> **To get user input in systems design, temporarily assign line managers to the central IS department.**

individual business units freely determine the number of systems developers their areas can profitably afford and absorb, and they choose their own project priorities.

For the striped-line model to work, it must be truly bidirectional. The IS organization needs to be open to influence by the corporate user community. A key technique to maintain a sense of realism about what users really want and need is to develop a rigorous charge-back mechanism for IS services. If the services of a given technical unit or specialty are not fully subscribed, cut head count. Don't adopt the common practice of burying allocated costs in data-center charges or corporate overhead. Charging services to corporate overhead is too easy a way to justify the unjustifiable—those things no user wants enough to pay for.

One company we studied goes a step further by pegging its internal IS rates for technical consultants to market prices rather than to internal costs. This forces the internal experts to be fully competitive with the best performers in the external market. Meanwhile, IS managers use whatever "profit" they accumulate to train staff in new technical skills, thus expanding their ability to help users in the future.

Other IS organizations heighten user-responsiveness by upgrading the service liaisons assigned to their business units. Some recruit representatives from user departments, software vendors, or high-powered consultancies. At one company, the top IS executive assigns his best applications developers to this role. And he has hired an independent company to conduct an annual survey of 1,800 users about IS department practices. When users complained in the first survey that the IS department was "difficult to do business with," he traced the problem to the complexity of the department's internal charge-back technique. So the staff worked hard to make its billing procedures explicit and then offered business unit managers on-line access to the details so computer expenditures could be clearly associated with the work of particular employees.

In a similar vein, one company strengthens the credibility of its information-technology billing practices by assigning rising stars from the controller's department to two-year stints within IS. During their tour of duty, visiting accountants prepare budgets, costing algorithms and charge-back formulas. Thus they can personally assure CPA peers in the divisions that the IS allocation methodology mirrors other standard company practices.

At a financial institution, high-potential line managers work in the central IS department for two years as part of their career development program. This means that the same people are designing applications who someday will have responsibility for their productive use. Some in the IS community complain that these "tourists" aren't around long enough to really learn the discipline of systems design. But these managers do become knowledgeable about real opportunities and impatient for results—which makes them perfect striped-line user representatives.

Such techniques make it possible for companies to capture the enormous benefits of IS centralization without losing the responsiveness to user needs that was the driving force behind decentralization. The result is an IS organization that combines the best of both worlds.

Reprint 90412

Managing the crises in data processing

A momentous change is taking place in the mission and function of corporate computing activities

Richard L. Nolan

Now that the experiences of many companies with advanced data processing (DP) systems can be analyzed, fresh and important observations can be made for the guidance of policy-making executives. For one thing, we can see the outlines of both the past and future, with six stages of DP growth standing out. Although no companies have yet entered stage 6, a few are approaching it, and a great many have entered the intermediate stages. Stage 3 produces a notable jump in already rapidly increasing computer costs; stage 4 features the rise to control of users of DP programs; and stages 5 and 6 feature the development and maturity of the new concept of data administration. For DP managers and program users, this evolution has significant implications. Planning, control, operations, technology, and costs—all are affected profoundly. Using the benchmarks described in this article, managers can see where their organizations stand in the evolutionary process. Turning to the guidelines described at the end, they can better understand how to manage the growth that lies ahead of them.

Mr. Nolan is chairman of Nolan, Norton & Company, Inc., Lexington, Massachusetts. Formerly he was associate professor of business administration at the Harvard Business School, where he taught courses in control and data processing and did extensive research in this field. He is the author or coauthor of a series of earlier HBR articles, including "Controlling the Costs of Data Services" (July-August 1977), "Business Needs a New Breed of EDP Manager" (March-April 1976), and "Managing the Four Stages of EDP Growth" (January-February 1974, with Cyrus F. Gibson).

The member of the corporation's steering committee did not mince words:

"I'm telling you I want the flow-of-goods computer-based system, and I am willing to pay for it. And you are telling me I can't have it after we have approved your fourth running annual budget increase of over 30%. If you can't provide the service, I'll get it outside. There are now reliable software companies around, and my people tell me that we should take seriously a proposal that we received from a large minicomputer vendor."

The reply of the vice president of information services was not well received:

"I'm at the edge of control. It isn't any longer a question of financial resources. My budget has grown from $30 million in 1975 to over $70 million in 1978. The technology is getting ultracomplex. I can't get the right people fast enough, let alone provide suitable space and connections to our sprawling computer network."

On returning to her office, the vice president knew that the steering committee member would be going ahead with the minicomputer. There was no way that the corporate technical staff could provide the flow-of-goods functions for the money or within the time frame that the minicomputer vendor had promised. Something was not right, even though she could not put her finger on it.

The vice president mused at the irony of it all. Five years ago she was brought in to set up a corporate computer utility after a similar period of poorly understood growth (that growth had been the undoing of her predecessor). Now key questions were being asked about a similar growth pattern of the data processing

(DP) budget, and she did not have the answers. She wished she did!

The plight of the vice president of information services is not singular. The rapid growth in DP services that many companies experienced in the mid- to late 1960s is occurring again in numerous companies. The resurgence is confusing.

The senior managements of some of these companies thought that the DP control structures put in place during the 1970s, such as chargeout, project management, and consolidation of computing activities under tight budgetary control, would contain any future budget growth. Nevertheless, the annual DP budget growth rates are exceeding 30%. Further, just the annual budget *increments* are equal to the total size of the budgets four or five years ago. The confused top executives of these companies are searching for answers to what underlies this growth. Is it good? Will it stop? What are the limits?

The answers are not obvious, but a probing of the status of the DP activities in different companies and of the current technological environment sheds light on the situation and provides insights into the management actions that are needed to prepare for and manage the growth.

Six stages of growth

Studies I have made during the 1970s of a series of companies—3 large corporations early in this decade, 35 companies several years ago, and then a large number of IBM customer concerns and other corporations since then—indicate the existence of six stages of growth in a company's DP function. These stages are portrayed in *Exhibit I*.

The scheme shown in this exhibit supersedes the four-stage concept I described in HBR in 1974.[1] The four stages described then continue to be valid, but the experience of recent years reveals a larger and more challenging picture.

This exhibit shows six stages of DP growth, from the inception of the computer into the organization to mature management of data resources. Through mid-stage 3, DP management is concerned with management of the computer. At some point in stage 3, there is a transition to management of data resources. This transition involves not only restructuring the DP organization but also installing new management techniques.

To understand the new picture, one must look at the growth in knowledge and technology, at organizational control, and at the shift from computer management to data resource management. I will consider each of these topics in turn.

Burgeoning of knowledge

Organizational learning and movement through the stages are influenced by the external (or professional) body of knowledge of the management of data processing as well as by a company's internal body of knowledge.

The external body of knowledge is a direct response to developments in information technology. It is concerned with developments in the theory of DP management as well as with the collective documented experiences of companies. The internal body of knowledge, however, benefits from the external body of knowledge but is primarily *experiential*—what managers, specialists, and operators learn firsthand as the system develops.

It is important to realize how greatly DP technology spurs the development and codification of an external, or professional, body of knowledge. For this reason a company that began to automate business functions in 1960 moved through the stages differently from a company that started to automate in 1970 or 1978. The information technology is different, and the extent of professional knowledge on how to manage the DP technology is much greater in the latter years. Not only is the external body of knowledge more sophisticated, but the information technology itself is more developed.

Control & slack

Organizational learning is influenced by the environment in which it takes place. One possible environment is what might be called "control"; a second might be called organizational "slack," a term coined by Richard M. Cyert and James G. March.[2]

In the *control* environment, all financial and performance management systems—including planning, budgeting, project management, personnel performance reviews, and chargeout or cost accounting systems—are used to ensure that DP activities are effective and efficient. In the *slack* environment, though, sophisticated controls are notably absent.

---

1. See my article, written with Cyrus F. Gibson, "Managing the Four Stages of EDP Growth," HBR January-February 1974, p. 76.

2. Richard M. Cyert and James G. March, "Organizational Factors in the Theory of Oligopoly," *Quarterly Journal of Economics*, February 1956, p. 44.

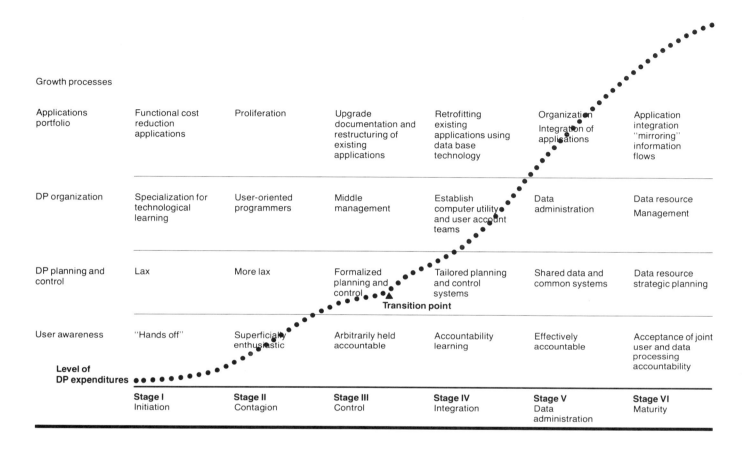

Exhibit I
Six stages of data processing growth

Instead, incentives to use DP in an experimental manner are present (for example, systems analysts might be assigned to users without any charge to the users' budgets).

When management permits organizational slack in the DP activities, it commits more resources to data processing than are strictly necessary to get the job done. The extra payment achieves another objective—nurturing of innovation. The new technology penetrates the business's multifunctional areas (i.e., production, marketing, accounting, personnel, and engineering). However, the budget will be looser, and costs will be higher. Management needs to feel committed to much more than just strict cost efficiency.

The balance between control and slack is important in developing appropriate management approaches for each stage of organizational learning. For example, an imbalance of high control and low slack in the earlier stages can impede the use of information technology in the organization; conversely, an imbalance of low control and high slack in the latter stages can lead to explosive DP budget increases and inefficient systems.

Exhibit II shows the appropriate balance of control and slack through the six stages. In stage 3 the orientation of management shifts from management of the computer to management of data resources. This shift, associated with introduction of the data base technology, explains the absence of entries in the computer columns after stage 3.

Shift in management emphasis

In stage 2 more and more senior and middle managers become frustrated in their attempts to obtain information from the company's computer-based systems to support decision-making needs. *Exhibit III* helps to explain the root of the problem. The exhibit is based on a fictional corporation that represents a kind of composite of the organizations studied. The spectrum of opportunities for DP equipment is called the "applications portfolio."

Exhibit II
Optimum balance of organizational slack and control

Stages	Organizational slack		Control		
	Computer	Data	Computer	Data	Objective of control systems
Stage 1	Low		Low		
Stage 2	High		Low		Facilitate growth
Stage 3	Low	Low	High	Low	Contain supply
Stage 4		High		Low	Match supply and demand
Stage 5		Low		High	Contain demand
Stage 6		High		High	Balance supply and demand

The triangle illustrates the opportunities for cost-effective use of data processing to support the various information needs in the organization. Senior management predominantly uses planning systems, middle management predominantly uses control systems, and operational management predominantly uses operational systems. At every level there are information systems that are uneconomic or unfeasible to automate, despite managers' desires for faster and better data.

In stage 1 in this organization, several low-level operational systems in a functional area, typically accounting, are automated. During stage 2 the organization encourages innovation and extensive application of the DP technology by maintaining low control and high slack. While widespread penetration of the technology is achieved by expanding into operational systems, problems are created by inexperienced programmers working without the benefit of effective DP management control systems. These problems become alarming when base-level systems cannot support higher-level systems—in particular, order processing, production control, and budgetary control systems. Maintenance of the existing, relatively poorly designed systems begins to occupy from 70% to 80% of the productive time of programmers and systems analysts.

Sometime in stage 3, therefore, one can observe a basic shift in orientation from management of the computer to management of the company's data resources. This shift in orientation is a direct result of analyses about how to put more emphasis, in expanding DP activities, on the needs of management control and planning as opposed to the needs of consolidation and coordination in the DP activities themselves. This shift also serves to keep data processing flexible to respond to management's new questions on control or ideas for planning.

As the shift is made, executives are likely to do a great deal of soul searching about how best to assimilate and manage data base technologies. The term "data administration" becomes common in conferences, and there is much talk about what data administration controls are needed.

But there is little effective action. I believe there is little action because the penetration of the technology is obviously low at its inception, and a combination of low control and high slack is the natural balanced environment to facilitate organizational learning. However, at the same time the seeds are being sown for a subsequent explosion in DP expenditures.

Stage 3 is characterized by rebuilding and professionalizing the DP activity to give it more standing in the organization. This stage is also characterized by initial attempts to develop user accountability for the DP expenditures incurred. Usually these attempts take the form of chargeouts for DP services. Unfortunately, both the conceptual and technical problems of implementing user accountability lead to confusion and alienation; real gains in accountability are not made. Nevertheless, the trends of DP charges in user budgets are rarely reversed.

Consequently, during stage 3 the users see little progress in the development of new control systems while the DP department is rebuilding, although they are arbitrarily held accountable for the cost of DP support and have little ability to influence the costs. Even the most stalwart users become highly frustrated and, in a familiar phrase, "give up on data processing."

Explosive growth

As stage 3 draws to a close, the DP department accomplishes its rebuilding and moves the data base and data communication technologies into several key application areas, such as order entry, general ledger, and materials requirements planning. In addition, the computer utility and network reach a point where high-quality services are being reliably provided to the users. When these accomplishments are realized, a subtle transition into stage 4 takes place.

Just when users have given up hope that data processing will provide anything new, they get interactive terminals and the various supports and assistance needed for using and profiting from data base technology. Already they have benignly accepted the cost of DP services. Now, with real value per-

Managing the crises in data processing 91

Exhibit III
Applications portfolio late in Stage II

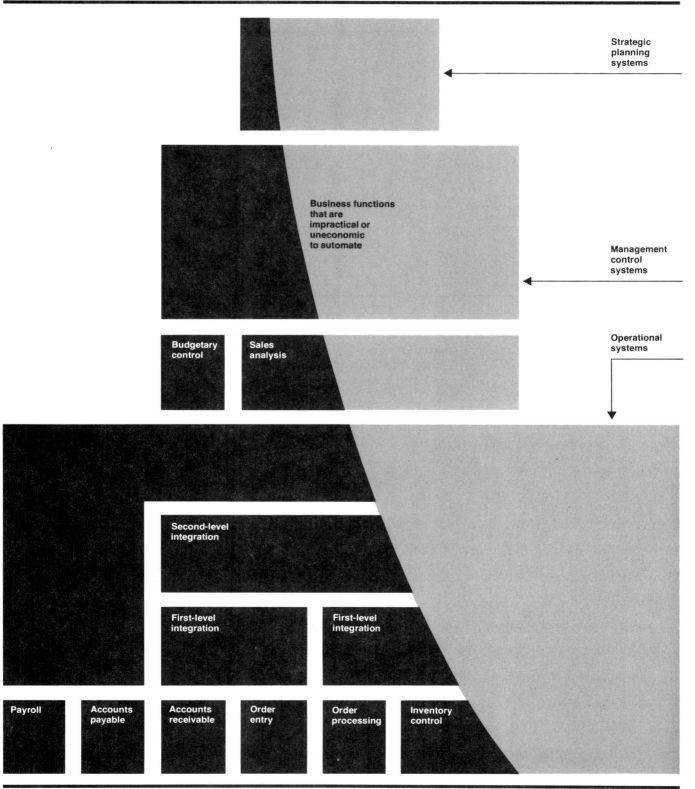

Note: An example of first-level integration is a purchase order application that uses order processing and inventory status information. An example of second-level integration is a vendor payment application that uses accounts payable and purchasing information.

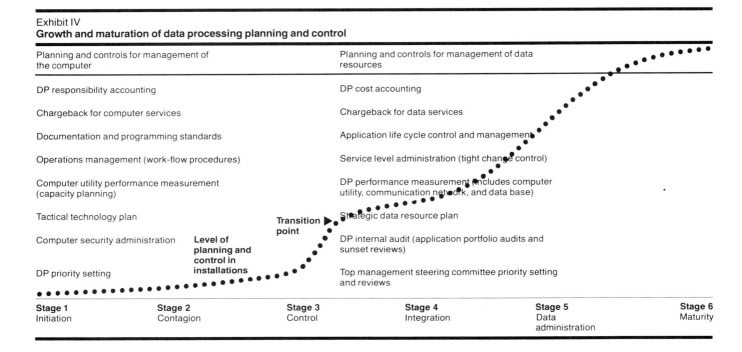

Exhibit IV
Growth and maturation of data processing planning and control

ceived, they virtually demand increased support and are willing to pay pretty much whatever it costs. This creates DP expenditure growth rates that may be reminiscent of those in stage 2, rates one may have thought would not be seen again.

It is important to underscore the fact that users perceive real value from data base applications and interactive terminals for data communication. In a recent study of one company with more than 1,500 applications, I found that users ranked their data base and interactive applications as far and away more effective than users of conventional or batch technology ranked their applications. This company has been sustaining DP expenditure growth rates of about 30% for the past four years. More important, the users of the new applications are demanding growth to the limits of the DP department's ability to expand.

The pent-up user demand of stage 3 is part of the reason. But a more important part of the reason is that the planning and control put in place in stage 3 are designed for *internal* management of the computer rather than for control of the growth in use of it and containment of the cost explosion. *Exhibit IV* shows the typical pattern of starting and developing internal and external (that is, user-managed) control systems. Late in stage 4, when exclusive reliance on the computer controls proves to be ineffective, the inefficiencies of rapid growth begin to create another wave of problems. The redundancy of data complicates the use of control and planning systems. Demands grow for better control and more efficiency.

In stage 5, data administration is introduced. During stage 6, the applications portfolio is completed, and its structure "mirrors" the organization and the information flows in the company.

Identifying the stage

How can executives determine what stage of development their corporate data processing is in? I have been able to develop some workable benchmarks for making such an assessment. Any one of the benchmarks taken alone could be misleading, but taken together these criteria provide a reliable image. I will describe some of the most useful benchmarks so management can gain a perspective on where it stands and on what developments lie down the road. For a visual portrayal of the benchmarks, see *Exhibit V*.

It is important to understand that a large multinational company may have divisions simultaneously representing stages 1, 2, 3, 4, and perhaps 5 or even 6. However, every division that I have studied has its DP concentrated in a particular stage. Knowledge of this stage provides the foundation for developing an appropriate strategy.

	Exhibit V **Benchmarks of the six stages**						
First-level analysis	DP expenditure benchmarks.	Tracks rate of sales growth.	Exceeds rate of sales growth.	Is less than rate of sales growth.	Exceeds rate of sales growth.	Is less than rate of sales growth.	Tracks rate of sales growth.
	Technology benchmarks.	100% batch processing.	80% batch processing. 20% remote job entry processing.	70% batch processing. 15% data base processing. 10% inquiry processing. 5% time-sharing processing.	50% batch and remote job entry processing. 40% data base and data communications processing. 5% personal computing. 5% minicomputer and microcomputer processing.	20% batch and remote job entry processing. 60% data base and data communications processing. 5% personal computing. 15% minicomputer and microcomputer processing.	10% batch and remote job entry processing. 60% data base and data communications processing. 5% personal computing. 25% minicomputer and microcomputer processing.
Second-level analysis	Applications portfolio.	There is a concentration on labor-intensive automation, scientific support, and clerical replacement.		Applications move out to user locations for data generation and data use.		Balance is established between centralized shared data/common system applications and decentralized user-controlled applications.	
	DP organization.	Data processing is centralized and operates as a "closed shop."		Data processing becomes data custodian. Computer utility established and achieves reliability. ◀ **Transition point**		There is organizational implementation of the data resource management concept. There are layers of responsibility for data processing at appropriate organizational levels.	
	DP planning and control.	Internal planning and control is installed to manage the computer. Included are standards for programming, responsibility accounting, and project management.				External planning and control is installed to manage data resources. Included are value-added user chargeback, steering committee, and data administration.	
Level of DP expenditures ▷	User awareness.	Reactive: End user is superficially involved. The computer provides more, better, and faster information than manual techniques.		Driving force: End user is directly involved with data entry and data use. End user is accountable for data quality and for value-added end use.		Participatory: End user and data processing are jointly accountable for data quality and for effective design of value-added applications.	
		Stage 1 Initiation	**Stage 2** Contagion	**Stage 3** Control	**Stage 4** Integration	**Stage 5** Data administration	**Stage 6** Maturity

First-level benchmarks

The first step is to analyze the company's DP expenditure curve by observing its shape and comparing its annual growth rate with the company's sales. A sustained growth rate greater than sales indicates either a stage 2 or 4 environment. Then, analyze the state of technology in data processing. If data base technology has been introduced and from 15% to 40% of the company's computer-based applications are operating using such technology, the company is most likely experiencing stage 4.

In the light of International Data Corporation's research on the number of companies introducing data base management systems technology in 1977 (shown in *Exhibit VI*), I believe that roughly half of the larger companies are experiencing stage 3 or 4. This is further corroborated by evidence that

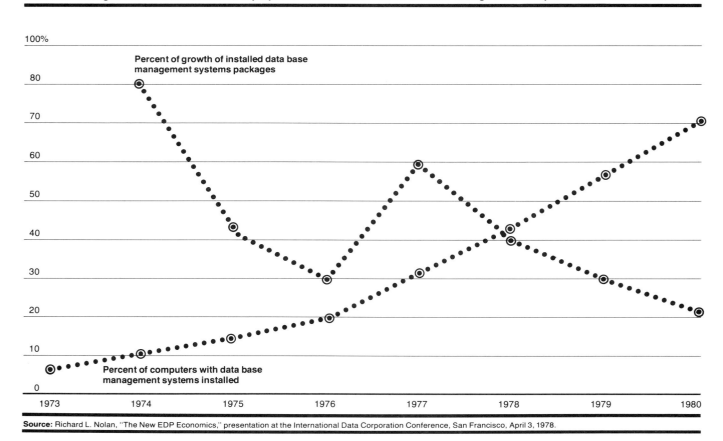

Exhibit VI
Data base management software installed and projected to be installed on IBM medium- to large-scale computers in the United States

Source: Richard L. Nolan, "The New EDP Economics," presentation at the International Data Corporation Conference, San Francisco, April 3, 1978.

1978 saw the largest annual percentage growth in the total DP budgets of U.S. companies—from $36 billion to an estimated $42 billion, or a 15½% increase.

As shown in Exhibit VI, about 55% of IBM installations in 1979 will have data base technology, compared with only about 20% in 1976. I feel that this means the explosive stage 4 in DP expenditures can be expected in the next two to five years in most companies; the increases may be somewhat moderated by continuance of the impressive technological advances that have improved prices and equipment performance.

Second-level benchmarks

The second step is to focus on the four growth processes shown in Exhibit V. Each major organizational unit of the company, such as a subsidiary, division, or department, should be listed. Then the growth processes associated with each organizational unit should be identified. For example, a decentralized subsidiary generally has all four growth processes, from expansion in the applications portfolio to an increase in employees' awareness of DP potentials and functions (see the left-hand side of Exhibit V). However, a division using the services of a corporate computer utility is likely to have only two of the growth processes—expansion in the applications portfolio and in user awareness.

Next, identify the stage (see the bottom of Exhibit V) of each of the growth processes associated with the organizational unit. Use growth as an example in the applications portfolio. The approach used for this process is similar to that for any of the processes. The procedure is as follows:

1. Define the set of business functions for the organizational unit that represents cost-effective opportunities to apply DP technology. I call this the "normative applications portfolio." It represents the business functions that would be receiving DP support if the company had achieved stage 6 maturity. Exhibit VII portrays such a scheme.

2. Taking each function in turn, indicate for each set of systems the support that data processing gives

Exhibit VII
Investment benchmarks for DP applications

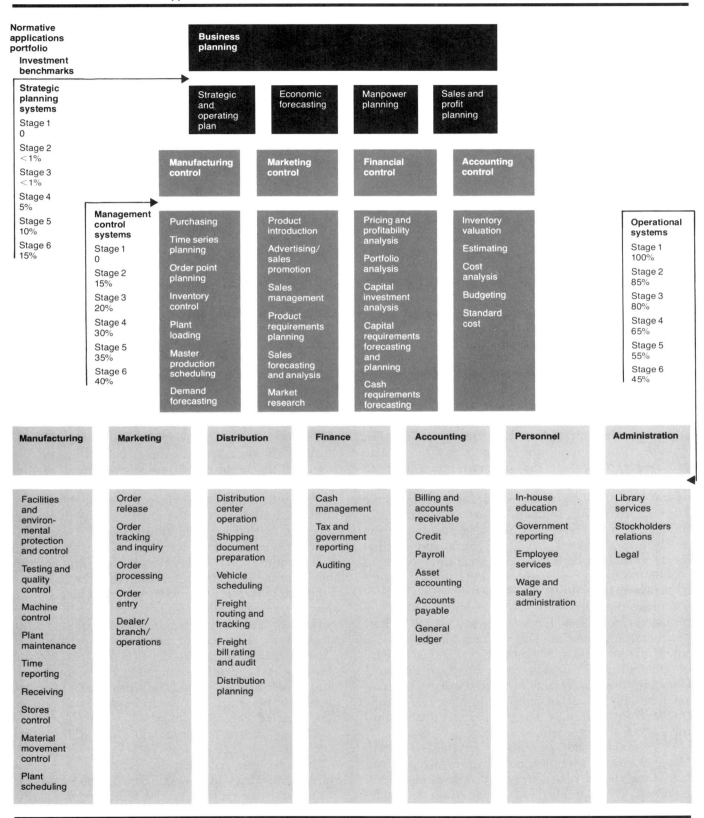

to the function in the organization. Ask, "What is it doing for our business?" I suggest doing this by shading the space for the function on the normative applications portfolio; use a ten-point scale to shade the function at 10%, 40%, 80% or whatever amount seems appropriate. Looking at all the shaded functions as a whole, judge the level of support given the system as a whole.

3. Then, match the support given the system as a whole with the benchmarks shown to the right of *Exhibit VII*. For instance, 80% support of operational systems, 20% support of management control systems, and just a faint trace of support for strategic planning systems would show the organization to be at stage 3.

4. Next, look for matches and mismatches between DP investment and the key functions that contribute to the company's return on investment or profitability. For example, if the company's business is manufacturing, and if half of the DP system investment goes to support accounting, a red flag is raised. The possibility of a mismatch between expenditure and need should be investigated.

After the functional assessment, one should conduct a technical assessment of the applications. The technical assessment gets at the concern of whether the DP activity is using current technology effectively. Benchmarks used include individual system ages, file structures, and maintenance resources required.

Again using a scheme like that described for *Exhibit VII*, compare the support given by data processing to the different corporate functions with the technical assessment. Are the DP systems old, or are the file structures out of date, or are there other shortcomings indicating that up-to-date technology is being neglected? Such neglect may be the result of managerial oversight, of a shortsighted desire to make a better annual profit showing, or of other reasons. In any case, it means that a portion of the company's assets are being sold off.

During the definition and assessment of the applications portfolios for a company, a DP "chart of accounts" is created. The business functions identified in the applications portfolio are the "objects of expenditures." Creating the chart of accounts is an important step in achieving the level of management sophistication required to effectively guide this activity through stages 4 and 5 and into the stage 6 environment.

So much for the applications portfolio analysis. Using the same sort of approach, management can turn next to the other growth processes shown in *Exhibit V* for second-level analysis. When the analysis is completed, management will have an overall assessment of the stage of the organization and of potential weaknesses in its ability for future growth.

If complete analyses of this type are made for all important organizations—divisional and functional—of the company, management will have a corporate-wide profile. *Exhibit VIII* is an example. Such a profile provides the foundation for developing an effective DP strategy.

Guidelines for action

In most sizable U.S. corporations, data processing is headed for an extremely rapid growth in the next five years. This growth is not necessarily bad; in fact, I believe that if the growth can be managed, it will be the most cost-effective growth experienced to date. Here are five guidelines for managing the growth successfully.

1. *Recognize the fundamental organizational transition from computer management to data resource management.*

With the introduction of data base technology in stage 3, an important shift in emphasis occurs—from managing the computer to managing the company's data resources. Obviously, this transition does not occur all at once. It appears first in the analysis of the late stage 2 applications portfolio and is a result of the requirement to restructure it so that applications can be tied together efficiently.

The transition also becomes apparent during the implementation of controls. Difficulties with charge-out systems that are computer-oriented cause management searches for alternative ways to achieve user accountability. This often leads to the conclusion that the user can be accountable for the functional support, but data processing must be accountable for management of shared data.

The key idea is to recognize the importance of the shift in management emphasis from the computer to data and then to develop applications and planning and control systems to facilitate the transition. Applications should be structured to share data; new planning and control systems should be data-oriented.

2. *Recognize the importance of the enabling technologies.*

The emerging information technologies are enabling companies to manage data economically. It is important to emphasize the word *economically*. What companies did only a few years ago in estab-

Exhibit VIII
One company's stage analysis

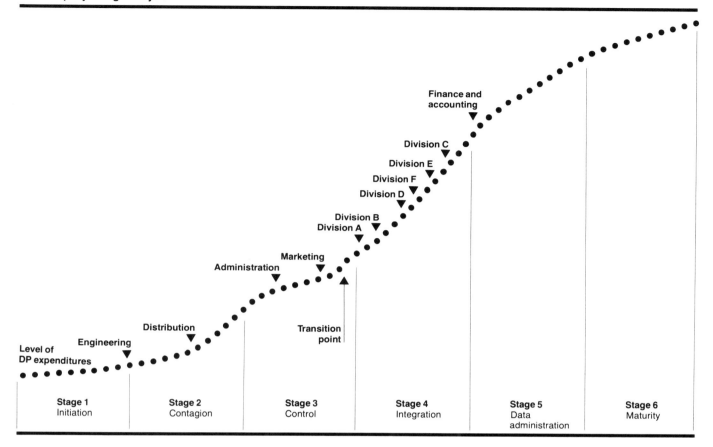

lishing large central DP utilities is no longer justifiable by economic arguments. Data resource management changes the economic picture.

Data base and data communication technologies are important from an organizational standpoint. Sprawling DP networks are enabling new approaches to management control and planning. We can now have multidimensional control structures such as function (e.g., manufacturing, marketing, and finance), product, project, and location. Managers and staff can be assigned to one or more of the dimensions. Through shared data systems, senior management can obtain financial and operating performance reports on any of the dimensions in a matter of hours after the close of the business day, month, quarter, or year.

Last but not least, developments in on-line terminals, minicomputers, and microcomputers are opening up new opportunities for doing business at the operational level. Airline reservation systems, for example, no longer stand alone in this area; we now can include point of sale (POS) for the retail industry, automated teller terminals (ATMs) for the banking industry, and plant automation for the manufacturing industry.

3. *Identify the stages of the company's operating units to help keep DP activities on track.*

A basic management tenet is: "If you can't measure it, you can't manage it." The applications portfolios of a company provide data processing with a chart of accounts. In the past, management lacked a generic and meaningful way to describe and track a DP activity—that is, to locate it in relation to the past and future. However, there is now a generic and empirically supported descriptive theory of the evolution of a DP activity—the stage theory. One can use this theory to understand where the company has come from, which problems were a result of weak management, and which problems arose from natural growth. More important, one can gain some insight into what the future may hold and then can try to develop appropriate management strategies that will accomplish corporate purposes.

4. *Develop a multilevel strategy and plan.*

Most DP departments have matured out of the "cottage industry" era. They have reached the point where they are woven into the operating fabric of their companies. There are many documented cases of the important impact that a computer failure of mere hours can have on a company's profitability.

Nevertheless, many DP departments continue to hold on to the cottage industry strategy of standing ready to serve any demands that come their way. This can have a disastrous effect when stage 4 begins to run its course. The extent and complexity of corporate activity make it impossible for data processing to be "all things to all users." Consequently, decisions will have to be made on what data processing will be—its priorities and purposes; when, where, and whom it will serve; and so on.

If the DP management makes these decisions without the benefit of an agreed-on strategy and plan, the decisions are apt to be wrong; if they are right, the rationale for them will not be adequately understood by users. If users do not understand the strategic direction of data processing, they are unlikely to provide support.

Development of an effective strategy and plan is a three-step process. *First*, management should determine where the company stands in the evolution of a DP function and should analyze the strengths and weaknesses that bear on DP strategies. *Second*, it should choose a DP strategy that fits in with the company's business strategy. And *third*, it should outline a DP growth plan for the next three to five years, detailing this plan for each of the growth processes portrayed in *Exhibit V*.

It is important to recognize that the plan resulting from this three-step process is, for most companies, an entry-level plan. Thus the plan cannot and should not be too detailed. It should provide the appropriate "blueprint" and goal set for each growth process to make the data processing more supportive of the overall business plan. It should also be a spark for all those in DP activities who want to make their work more significant and relevant to corporate purposes.

5. *Make the steering committee work.*

The senior management steering committee is an essential ingredient for effective use of data processing in the advanced stages. It provides direction to the strategy formulation process. It can reset and revise priorities from time to time to keep DP programs moving in the right direction.

From my observation, I think that the steering committee should meet on a quarterly basis to review progress. This would give enough time between meetings for progress to be made in DP activities and would allow the committee to monitor progress closely. Plan progress and variances can make up the agenda of the review sessions.

Reprint 79206

Ideas for Action

Edited by
Timothy B. Blodgett

Save your information system from the experts

Richard S. Rubin

All is not well with information systems. But sometimes it's hard for managers to tell what's gone wrong. Consider the following story:

An East Coast-based company that built automated teller machines ordered spare parts that were manufactured and stockpiled on the West Coast. It then shipped the parts East and stored them again on the East Coast. When the parts were shipped East, they became an expense item on the company books in the West. An automated inventory system for the East Coast warehouse seemed the obvious way to keep track of parts movement and reorder requirements.

Three years after the system was installed, management found that the orders for parts had been expanding exponentially even though the parts were not actually being used for repairs in the field. The inventory system had gone haywire. What had happened?

When management finally audited the system it found that:

1   The automated system and the physical inventory were completely out of sync. They had practically nothing in common.

2   The program instructions could not be changed without the original programmers, and they were unavailable.

3   The sets of figures in both the West and the East were dynamic, on-line data and could be reconciled only for current shipments. The system could not account for past shipments. Therefore the original amount of inventory shipped, which was expensed on the company books, was impossible to reconcile with inventory system totals.

4   Only one person in the warehouse knew how to operate the system; when that person was away, the paperwork piled up.

5   The system's language was suitable only for minicomputers, and expansion of the warehouse would require on-line computers; therefore the warehouse could not be expanded.

6   The warehouse systems for shipping had many security breaches.

The experts, it seems, had built the system without keeping management informed. And management didn't ask questions. Nothing is new about problems with information processing. What is new is that a class of technicians has managed to remove large data processing expenditures from the control of corporate management and the rule of common sense. In the above case, warehouse management didn't even know about the imbalance or that unneeded parts were being ordered.

How could management have monitored the system or known when it had gone awry? Three options are possible. First, management could have ordered an information system (IS) audit from the very beginning that required adherence to a system development life cycle by testing the new system against the old. The exorbitant reorder costs would have been saved, proper documentation would have removed the need to rewrite the system, and the choice of a software language capable of migrating from minicomputers to a mainline system would have allowed expansion. Second, upper managers could have assigned a project team member to report to them and give them the details they needed. Third, a member of the management team overseeing the project could have noted where things were headed and might have been able to correct the situation.

Tentative solutions

After becoming familiar with precarious situations like these—in which experts build information systems helter-skelter while management remains oblivious—most managers have decided that they need some way to track the IS team's activities. At first, they had thought conventional finance auditors could make some sense out of all this. Wrong. When finance people come into a data processing center, they ask basic questions like, "You really prepare a budget every year, don't you?"

Ludicrous findings often result from these audits. One disclosure said, for example, that "during a tape inventory it was found that Tape 319 was misfiled." Such simplistic statements make data processing people laugh. Professionals with no training in data processing are hired to audit pro-

Richard Rubin is a telecommunications manager at Citibank in New York City and is also an assistant professor of computer science at Pace University.

© 1986 by the President and Fellows of Harvard College, all rights reserved.

fessionals who have spent years learning a subject that is an art, not a science.

The solution was a long time coming. In many corporations, people with both programming and accounting backgrounds were hired to communicate between data processing people and upper management. The company hoped that meaningful, unbiased advice would result and that top management would be able to make commonsense decisions on high-cost concerns. The difficulties with this approach, however, were twofold:

1   Where to find enough people with backgrounds in both data processing and management.
2   How to build loyalty to nontechnical upper management into the IS team's reporting structure.

Companies can overcome these difficulties in one of three ways, as I indicated in the automated warehouse example. They can use IS auditors (people trained in both accounting and programming), a member of the data processing project team, or a member of an upper management reporting committee.

Information auditor. To prevent IS chaos, management needs controls. In the past, such controls prevented defalcation and intentional wrongdoing and ensured that totals balanced out. Now they are needed to ensure the maintenance of project development standards. IS auditors may be able to keep management's standards in place. In the last decade, many companies have accepted and used IS auditors. In the United States, each of the Big Eight accounting firms has its own IS audit people available for clients.

Unfortunately, IS auditors have been used mostly for data center hardware reviews. Such audits made more sense when hardware constituted 70% of the costs of running a data center. As the cost of hardware dropped dramatically every year, the cost ratio reversed. Today 70% of the data processing budget goes to software development, maintenance, and enhancement. With this changed focus, a company needs to ensure that its IS is on track. Management needs to know that its standards are being adhered to—all along the way.

Companies commonly use a life-cycle approach for tracking new-systems projects. A system's cycle flows as follows: feasibility study, information analysis, system design, program development, procedures and forms development, acceptance testing, conversion, and operation and maintenance standards.

This step-by-step procedure seems simple enough. Wouldn't any reasonable project leader follow it? Not by a long shot. By skipping this procedure, project leaders save time, effort, and money for themselves, but not for the company. When the project team eventually disperses, who is left with the undocumented, incomplete project? The company is or, I might say, you are! By ordering rigid adherence to system development life-cycle standards, the company can overcome project leaders' reluctance to comply.

"Upper level managers need an interpreter to make rational decisions about programming costs."

A good feasibility study done at the outset can help keep high standards throughout the project's life and can save untold grief later. This study should include both the company's needs and the ramifications for the proposed system if key people leave or if, for whatever reason, a software house stops supporting the package. The study should also ask what impact system failure would have on the business.

Reporting team member. The second option, having a project member report on the ongoing project, prevents a crisis months or years into the project, when an outsider must make a crucial judgment that could take as many months or years. Requiring the team member who reports to the project leader to report midproject to a management vice president can fend off disaster. The team members may consider the reporting member a viper in the nest. Resistance to change can be a real hurdle; explaining that the review will improve the system may help employees expect and accept the reporting process.

Management should stress that the reporting structure was changed not to put blame on anyone but to identify the project's weaknesses. Reporting by a project member will provide the most accurate and plentiful information on a project's status. Management must make the reporting member feel that the report is a real contribution to the project. If the project's creators have not properly documented it along the way, when they leave, the corporation will have bought nothing.

Management committee member. The third option is involvement of a member of an upper management committee in the project from the beginning. What the member does not know about the project's technical aspects, he or she can make up for in employing good management processes like ensuring proper documentation and ensuring that internal feuding or rivalry does not jeopardize the outcome. Such a person will act as an early warning system against inevitable costly overruns.

A committee member may also be able to spot expensive technical solutions proposed for problems that do not require them. Technicians often think only in terms of technical solutions. If, for example, only four pieces of information are transferred to a location per day, an elaborate teleprocessing system is hardly required to send them. The mail or a messenger could do it.

Common sense to the rescue

Each option for monitoring systems projects has its merits. The only one that features someone who formally studies and has broad experience in review work is the IS auditor. The project team member is particularly useful on a very technical project not only in providing information to technically uninformed managers but also for having such specialized skills as knowing how to program in CICS Cobol. But such a person cannot give a well-rounded review of all aspects of a project, like emergency backup procedures or the security system. A management team member working inside as headquarters' liaison can take direct decision-making responsibility based on firsthand information that will be useful in project revision, but the person may lack technical skills.

To make rational decisions about programming costs, upper level managers need an interpreter. Data processing has its own language, but once past the language barrier, managers can make rational decisions based on common sense. IS auditors are among the best interpreters available. Let them do the fieldwork and attend all the meetings held in system development projects. Do rely on common sense when the results from the audit are in.

Of the three options, the IS audit is the most formalized approach and will ultimately require the growth and support of a new profession. Some of the top IS audit talents from various companies in the New York City area have met at EDP auditors' meetings and admitted that standards are not uniform or generally accepted industry-wide and that the establishment of such standards is a needed first step. With the EDP Auditors Association, Pace University, and other organizations publishing, giving instruction in, and agreeing on methodologies and a common body of knowledge, an IS auditor's profession is in sight. As other schools start such graduate programs, a common body of knowledge may emerge.

Always remember what you originally wanted the system to accomplish. Having the latest, greatest system and a flashy data center to boot is not what data processing is supposed to be all about. It is supposed to help the bottom line, not hinder it.

If a new software system comes out that promises to do everything you want, wait until all the pieces of the system are fully operational and functioning. Let some other companies install the system first and go through the anguish of debugging it. Be conservative. Does your company really need the latest? If it will add nothing to the functioning of your primary business—say, producing springs—then common sense should tell you that it isn't necessary to be on the technology's cutting edge. If all this sounds basic, it is.

Management has a few defenses against IS chaos: the use of system development life cycles, excellent documentation, and strict standards that are enforced. Above all these, though, is an overriding sense of innate proportion and common sense in upper management. Without them, the profits of most companies will eventually be lavished in vain on the latest and greatest state-of-the-art technology in data processing and programming extravaganzas.

Reprint 86412

Jesse James at the terminal

William Atkins

The new computing environment presents many opportunities for a different kind of highway robbery

This cautionary tale of computer derring-do shows how a present-day miscreant almost gets away with a $2 million heist before his company knows something is missing. Embedded in this scenario are the outlines of the typical computer crime. Though the fictional TechneeCorp had installed some state-of-the-art security measures, it had failed to implement several vital personnel procedures. At almost every stage of his plot to defraud Technee, the criminal could have – and should have – been caught. As happens in many computer capers today, the story's ending turns almost on a quirk of fate.

Mr. Atkins, national director, advanced technology, Touche Ross & Company, New York, has worked with information systems for 25 years. As a consultant during the last 18 years, he has worked with clients in all segments of the private and public sectors. He is the coauthor of three books on information systems development and management.

Illustrations by Ronald Searle.

Jesse James was angry. Seething. How could they pass him over for promotion again? Jesse had been sure that the company would long ago have recognized and rewarded his ingenuity. But it hadn't, and he was mad. If they weren't going to give him what he deserved, he'd get it himself.

If one could trust appearances, Jesse was the very model of a modern systems analyst. At 29, he had put in six years with TechneeCorp. He came in early and stayed late. He even took his personal computer home so he could work nights and weekends. He had learned the company's computer system quickly, and just as quickly he had devised ways to bypass the controls and make it work better.

Though Jesse fit the picture of the up and coming computer professional, he prided himself on his connections to his dashing and courageous predecessor, the intrepid robber of banks and trains. He had the name, of course, although his name, Jesse James Wheeler, came from his two grandfathers, so the conjunction happened entirely by chance. He also had the cleverness. His knowledge of TechneeCorp's computer system would bring him more money than a gun ever could.

Jesse's daring namesake had always sought to justify his banditry on grounds of persecution. Moreover, the original James gang used to brag that it had never robbed a friend, a preacher, a Southerner, or a widow. Jesse decided that he would be as considerate. He would not steal from anyone but the faceless corporation.

He decided to set up a fictitious vendor-payable account in the computer, then transfer payments directly to his bank account.

Maxim:
When information systems are involved, beware of disgruntled employees.

Like many large companies, TechneeCorp maintained extensive EDP operations with centralized and distributed computer systems as well as a flock of microcomputers wired into both. Management understood the value of its electronic treasure trove and had taken steps to protect it.

Special access-control software allowed terminal users—identified by user codes and passwords—to access only records for which they were authorized and to perform only specific, authorized functions such as reading files or adding or deleting information. The software could also limit the amount of information available to each authorized user, restrict the central computer to private, secured phone lines, or allow access to certain terminals only. Perhaps most important, the software kept records of who accessed what, from which terminal, and when.

Jesse had known for some time that the specialized audit software existed, but its secrets were closely guarded by the auditors themselves. They caused his biggest worry: since he didn't know where the system's traps lay, he couldn't be certain of avoiding them. He decided to minimize the risk of being caught. During the robbery he would leave a little "present"—a special program that would cover his tracks by eliminating any record of the payment transactions.

While working on his microcomputer, Jesse had noticed an inordinately long wait after he signed on with his user code and password before the central computer responded that he was logged on and could proceed. He decided to ask his supervisor about this. "Not to worry," said Matt, "it's just security. The system cuts you off. It drops the line, so to speak, and dials you back. Or, I should say, it dials back the phone number you should be using. That's how it knows every terminal tapping into it is right where it ought to be." Matt also told Jesse that every supervisor had a frequently changed password that allowed access to the "secured" systems. He had designed many of these features himself and was justly proud of them.

Maxim:
All employees must be sensitive to security.

TechneeCorp's security managers had done all they and the insurance company had deemed necessary. They knew about even more sophisticated and exotic access-control devices—there were gadgets that scanned potential users' fingerprints, voiceprints, even the blood vessels in their retinas—but they came at a price TechneeCorp wasn't willing to pay.

Jesse needed a password that would give him access to supervisory functions because to divert funds to a fictitious account, he first had to be able to create that account. He needed a partner and he found Frank—a computer operator with a bit of a gambling problem. Nothing serious, just a few hundred each week. Frank had no love for Technee either. But he did have a way of getting the master password list.

Maxim:
Investigate your computer personnel before hiring, and be alert to evidence of such personal problems as compulsive gambling and alcoholism.

Frank used to work at Technee's world headquarters; in fact, somewhat against his wishes, he'd been transferred to Jesse's eastern region office in Newark only a few weeks before. So nobody thought much about it when Frank showed up at WHQs' impressive office complex in Stamford, Connecticut. The sensitive nature of TechneeCorp's business necessitated its state-of-the-art physical security system. Both outside and inside the modern structure, surveillance cameras silently scanned every movement, day and night.

Frank knew the cameras had picked him up the minute he pulled into the employee lot. But he didn't care. His parking pass was still on his windshield. And his ID badge hanging from his lapel cleared him to enter both the building and the computer installation.

Maxim:
Keep all personnel records and privileges up to date.

"Hi, Frank," said Butch, smiling from ear to ear. Butch was Technee's oldest security guard. Even though he knew Frank had been transferred, he didn't bother to check whether he should be there. After all, he'd known him for three years.

To get the password list, Frank needed to enter the computer installation. He could do that the same way he always had—by punching a four-digit code into a key pad on the door panel. True, they had changed the code since Frank left, but getting the new code wouldn't be that difficult.

Frank simply wandered into the programming section. "Hey!" he yelled at no one in particular. "What's the code this week?" "It's 313," came the reply from a frosted glass cubicle. Like all the codes, this was simply a telephone area code. Following standard procedure, Frank prefixed a "1," punched 1-313, and entered the installation.

The main computer was, as befitted its delicate eyes, ears, and sinuses, enclosed in a scrubbed-clean room to the right, sealed off from the printers with their nasty dust, confetti, and vibrations. Frank turned left into the print room, and, after a few minutes of ruffling through the output reports that awaited pickup, found what he wanted—the list of supervisor password codes and the special terminal passwords.

"I've got the passwords," thought Frank in silent triumph. "But I couldn't have done it if those people hadn't helped me. In the end, people are what's important."

Maxim:
Keep all security codes strictly secret.

During his six years with Technee, Jesse had learned about many of the complete operation's security features. Quite early on, he had noticed that, whereas each vendor account number had only six digits, the order entry group keyed seven numbers into the system.

He knew that the seventh digit was a check digit—part of the security system—and to create a new account he would have to devise a correct check digit of his own. Since he knew many of the accounts' full numbers, Jesse could use his own computer and a simple program to arrive at the numerical process that unlocked all the account numbers. Having the check digit process and the passwords, he could construct new account numbers that the system would readily accept.

Jesse's first assault on TechneeCorp was a failure. The kind of failure, in fact, that would have bloodied, if not killed, his train-robbing namesake. As he had often done before, Jesse brought home his personal computer. Remembering what Matt had told him about the callback security feature, he first took the precaution of forwarding his office phone calls automatically to his home phone. "No control device exists," he thought smugly, "that can tell when a call's being forwarded." Using the password list Frank had given him, he logged on and entered Matt's supervisor code.

He headed straight for the program for creating new accounts—and directly into a very expensive, very subtle, and very clever trap. For though the system seemed to be following his instructions obediently, in reality it was doing nothing he asked and was all the while recording his every move. Jesse had been snared by a state-of-the-art audit software package that gave him access to a set of false files and freedom to do as he wanted.

To give due credit to his thespian talents, it must be noted that Jesse showed no trace of panic when the chief security officer from WHQ called him into Matt's office the next afternoon. There on the desk was the evidence—a printout declaring:

```
OPERATOR IDENTIFIED AS
SUPERVISOR 31688
ON INVALID SUPERVISOR
TERMINAL 5479,
TELEPHONE NUMBER 555-2564,
ACCESSED THIS PROGRAM
FROM 1954:50 TO 2003:25,
6.19.85.
```

Matt, of course, denied using Jesse's terminal—as did Jesse himself. The building guards could not say for sure that Jesse had taken a terminal home the previous night. He was off the hook; there was no way they could prove he—and not someone else—had used his terminal.

The experience, though almost fatal, proved immensely valuable to Jesse, for now he possessed a piece of vital knowledge—namely, that there was another level of security to be breached. The company had installed a security system on the terminals themselves, so that not all terminals could do all things.

Jesse needed a supervisor's terminal. And he needed it on a Thursday so that Friday morning the accounts payable program would make a payment to "his" account.

Maxim:
Sophisticated security software systems are only as reliable as
the people who guard them.

Another long day at the office. Time to scoop up the micro and lug it off to do some homework. At the employee exit, Danny, the security guard, was just getting ready for a restful evening. "Hey, Danny! My computer's on the fritz and I've got a boatload of work tonight. How's about letting me into Matt's office so I can use his? He said I could use it anytime.

Danny had never paid much attention to those typewriter-TV screen things; seen one, seen 'em all. Jesse, of course, knew better. He needed Matt's five-star Supervisor I with circuit boards that would make that audit software program roll out the red carpet. While picking up the machine, he set the call-forward to his home phone. With unusual good cheer, he wished Danny a good evening. He himself intended to have one.

Jesse James at the terminal 107

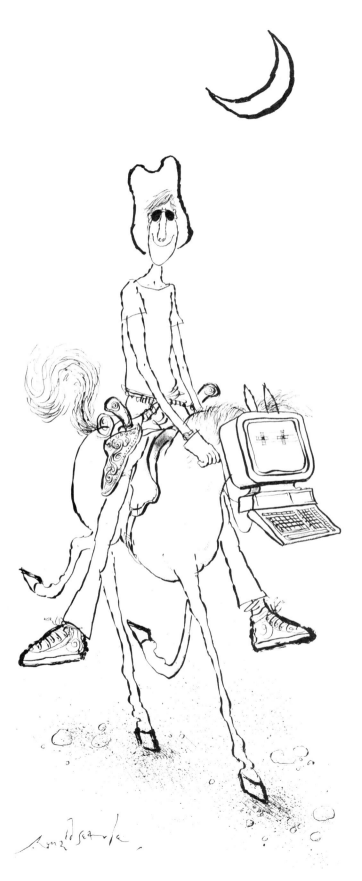

It is 11:30 p.m. Jesse is seated comfortably in his bedroom. His elaborate preparations are behind him. It had all come down to this: the silent predator with his elemental weapons—Jesse James with a terminal and a modem.

It had all been rather simple. Using everything he had learned at Technee, Jesse tapped into its central computer and created an account in his name. He had noted carefully all the necessary numbers: account, check digit, vendor, bank, ABA transit, and bank account. Carefully, he read from his notes. By simply inputting the appropriate purchase order and balances, he initiated next-cycle payment transactions totaling $2 million. He then applied a finishing touch of criminal acumen: a little time bomb—a program that would remove all evidence.

Jesse didn't sleep a wink that night. He alternated between imagining how he would spend such an enormous amount of money—villas, yachts, wining and dining, gambling—and gloating over how he had beaten the billion-dollar TechneeCorp with all its policies, procedures, and precautions.

In the morning, Jesse panicked. The long night had taken its toll. When the alarm had sounded he had turned it off automatically and fallen asleep. Now it was 7:15 a.m. He got dressed quickly, grabbed the computer, and dashed for his car. Usually at work no later than 7 a.m., Jesse knew that Matt came in about 8.

Practically knocking someone over, he rushed breathless up to Bob at the guard desk. "Is Matt in yet?" he asked. Jesse's mind was racing as he tried to figure out what he could say if Matt was already there. The monitoring system would show that there was no problem with Jesse's terminal. How would he be able to explain taking Matt's?

"Haven't seen him," replied Bob. The answer seemed to take an eternity to sink in. He just stood there. "Thank goodness," he said finally. He didn't even notice the stares Bob and the other person gave him.

Jesse, explaining to Bob that he had used Matt's computer because his was broken, got him to unlock Matt's door. He set the machine down on the desk, connected it to the electrical outlet, plugged in the telephone jack, and cancelled the call-forwarding instruction. "What presence of mind!" he thought. "Switzerland, here I come."

Jane Clades, a waitress in TechneeCorp's executive dining room, hadn't missed a day since the doors opened at this branch just over nine years ago. She was proud to be part of TechneeCorp and its success; she felt she belonged.

She read the monthly employee bulletin regularly and had been interested recently in the article entitled "Security: Everyone's Responsibility." She liked the fact that TechneeCorp believed its first line of security was its people. The article emphasized a family image: everyone pulling together and all keeping alert. Jane also liked the friendly chief security officer from WHQ who wrote the article; he'd visit at least once every few months and always stopped in the restaurant for a cup of coffee.

Jane didn't like Jesse James's bumping into her that morning without one word of apology. He hadn't hurt her, but his bad manners annoyed her. She also kept thinking about how nervous he looked when he asked the guard to let him into a supervisor's office. Why did he need to get into that office in such a hurry? Why couldn't he just wait?

Jane told the short-order chef what had happened. As they talked, the more she thought Jesse James had behaved suspiciously, and the more the chef encouraged her to do something.

Telling herself she had nothing to lose and encouraged by the article she had read, Jane called TechneeCorp's chief security officer and told him her story.

Even with considerable assistance, security personnel took more than 36 hours of work around the clock to uncover enough evidence to indicate embezzlement. (If Jesse hadn't applied his time bomb program, they could have reconstructed events in a few hours.) Because they had no way to prove the crime, the rest was up to the chief security officer.

Waiting for his taxi to the airport, Jesse checked his luggage. It looked like everything was in order. In just 90 minutes, he would be on the plane; in a few hours, he would be skiing and beginning to enjoy the $2 million. He heard the door bell and, with a smile of anticipation, picked up his skis, boots, and the suitcase, and opened the door. Jesse's face turned white, his mouth went dry, and his legs began to shake. The last person he expected to see on his doorstep at high noon on a Sunday was the chief security officer of TechneeCorp.

"Do you know how you're going to spend it all yet?" asked the officer. Jesse couldn't believe he had made a mistake. He had to know where he had gone wrong. "I don't understand," he blurted out without thinking. "How did you work it out?"

The officer's bluff had worked.

And Frank had been right. In the final analysis, people make the difference.

Reprint 85401

HBR CASE STUDY

Dominion-Swann management acquires technology to support employees — or control them?

The Case of the Omniscient Organization

by Gary T. Marx

The following is an excerpt from Dominion-Swann Industries' 1995 Employee Handbook. DS is a $1 billion diversified company, primarily in the manufacture of electrical components for automobiles. This section of the handbook was prepared by the corporate director of personnel, in consultation with the human resource management firm SciexPlan Inc.

Dominion-Swann's new workplace: Hope for industry through technology

We are a technology-based company. We respect our employees, whose knowledge is the core of the technological enterprise. We care about the DS community. We value honesty, informed consent, and unfettered scientific inquiry. Our employees understand company strategy. They are free to suggest ways to improve our performance. We offer handsome rewards for high productivity and vigorous participation in the life of our company. Committed to science, we believe in careful experimentation and in learning from experience.

Since 1990, we have instituted changes in our work environment. The reasons for change were clear enough from the start. In 1990, DS faced an uncertain future. Our productivity and quality were not keeping pace with overseas competition. Employee turnover was up, especially in the most critical part of our business — automotive chips, switches, and modules. Health costs and work accidents were on the rise. Our employees were demoralized. There were unprecedented numbers of thefts from plants and offices and leaks to competitors about current research. There was also a sharp rise in drug use. Security personnel reported unseemly behavior by company employees not only in our parking lots and athletic fields but also in restaurants and bars near our major plants.

In the fall of 1990, the company turned to SciexPlan Inc., a specialist in employee-relations management in worldwide companies, to help develop a program for the radical restructuring of the work environment. We had much to learn from the corporate cultures of overseas competitors and were determined to benefit from the latest advances in work-support technology. The alternative was continued decline and, ultimately, the loss of jobs.

Frankly, there was instability while the program was being developed and implemented. Some valued employees quit and others took early retirement. But widespread publicity about our efforts drew to the program people who sincerely sought a well-ordered, positive environment. DS now boasts a clerical, professional, and factory staff which understands how the interests of a successful company correspond with the interests of individual employees. To paraphrase psychologist William James, "When the community dies, the individual withers." Such sentiments, we believe, are as embedded in Western traditions as in Eastern; they are the foundation of world community. They are also a fact of the new global marketplace.

The fundamentals

Since 1990, productivity per worker is up 14%. Sales are up 23%, and the work force is down 19%. Employees' real income is up 18%, due in large part to our bonus and profit-sharing plans. Many of these efficiencies can be attributed to reform of our factories' production technologies. But we can be proud to have been ahead of our time in the way we build our corporate spirit and use social technologies.

At DS four principles underlie work-support restructuring:

1. Make the company a home to employees. Break down artificial and alienating barriers between work and home. Dissolve, through company initiative, feelings of isolation. Great companies are made by great people; all employee behavior and self-development counts.

Gary T. Marx is professor of sociology at Massachusetts Institute of Technology. He is author of Undercover: Police Surveillance in America *(University of California Press, 1988).*

2. Hire people who will make a continuing contribution. Bring in people who are likely to stay healthy and successful, people who will be on the job without frequent absences. Candor about prospective employees' pasts may be the key to the company's future.

3. Technical, hardware-based solutions are preferable to supervision and persuasion. Machines are cheaper, more reliable, and fairer than managers. Employees want to do the right thing; the company wants nothing but this and will give employees all the needed technical assistance. Employees accept performance evaluation from an impartial system more readily than from a superior and appreciate technical solutions that channel behavior in a constructive direction.

4. Create accountability through visibility. Loyal employees enjoy the loyalty of others. They welcome audits, reasonable monitoring, and documentary proof of their activities, whether of location, business conversations, or weekly output. Once identified, good behavior can be rewarded, inappropriate behavior can be improved.

These principles have yielded an evolving program that continues to benefit from the participation and suggestions of our employees. The following summary is simply an introduction. The personnel office will be pleased to discuss any aspect of community performance or breaches of company policy in detail with employees. (You may call for an appointment during normal business hours at X-2089.)

Entry-level screening

As a matter of course and for mutual benefit, potential employees are screened and tested. We want to avoid hiring people whose predictive profile—medications, smoking, obesity, debt, high-risk sports, family crises—suggests that there will be serious losses to our community's productivity in the future.

Job applicants volunteer to undergo extensive medical and psychological examinations and to provide the company with detailed personal information and records, including background information about the health, lifestyle, and employment of parents, spouses, siblings, and close friends. Company associates seek permission to make discreet searches of various databases, including education, credit, bankruptcy and mortgage default, auto accident, driver's license suspension, insurance, health, worker's compensation, military, rental, arrest, and criminal activity.

The company opposes racial and sexual discrimination. DS will not check databases containing the names of union organizers or those active in controversial political causes (whether on the right or the left). Should the company's inquiry unwittingly turn up such information, it is ignored. We also use a résumé verification service.

Since our community is made up of people, not machines, we have found it useful to compare physiological, psychological, social, and demographic factors against the profiles of our best employees. Much of this analysis has been standardized. It is run by SciexPlan's expert system, INDUCT.

Community health

We want employees who are willing to spend their lives with the company, and we care about their long-term health. The company administers monthly pulmonary tests in behalf of the zero-tolerance smoking policy. Zero tolerance means lower health insurance premiums and improved quality of life for all employees.

In cooperation with Standar-Hardwick, one of the United States's most advanced makers of medical equipment and a valued customer, we've developed an automated health monitor. These new machines, used in a private stall and activated by employee thumbprint, permit biweekly urine analysis and a variety of other tests (blood pressure, pulse, temperature, weight) without the bother of having to go to a health facility. This program has received international attention: at times, it has been hailed; at times, severely criticized. People at DS often express surprise at the fuss. Regular monitoring of urine means early warning against diabetes and other potentially catastrophic diseases—and also reveals pregnancy. It also means that we can keep a drug-free, safe environment without subjecting people to the in-

DRAWINGS BY CHUCK MORRIS

dignities of random testing or the presence of an observer.

The quality environment

Drawing on SciexPlan's research, our company believes that the physical environment is also important to wellness and productivity. Fragrant aromas such as evergreen may reduce stress; the smell of lemon and jasmine can have a rejuvenating effect. These scents are introduced to all work spaces through the air-conditioning and heating systems. Scents are changed seasonally.

Music is not only enjoyable to listen to but can also affect productivity. We continually experiment with the impact of different styles of music on an office's or plant's aggregate output. Since psychologists have taught us that the most serious threat to safety and productivity is stress, we use subliminal messages in music such as "safety pays," "work rapidly but carefully," and "this company cares." Personal computers deliver visual subliminals such as "my world is calm" or "we're all on the same team."

At the start of each month, employees are advised of message content. Those who don't want a message on their computers may request that none be transmitted—no questions asked. On the whole, employees who participate in the program feel noticeably more positive about their work. Employees may borrow from our library any one of hundreds of subliminal tapes, including those that help the listener improve memory, reduce stress, relax, lose weight, be guilt-free, improve self-confidence, defeat discouragement, and sleep more soundly.

On the advice of SciexPlan's dieticians, the company cafeteria and dining room serve only fresh, wholesome food prepared without salt, sugar, or cholesterol-producing substances. Sugar- and caffeine-based, high-energy snacks and beverages are available during breaks, at no cost to employees.

Work monitoring

Monitoring system performance is our business. The same technologies that keep engines running at peak efficiency can keep the companies that make engine components running efficiently too. That is the double excitement of the information revolution.

At DS, we access more than 200 criteria to assess productivity of plant employees and data-entry personnel. These criteria include such things as the quantity of keystroke activity, the number of errors and corrections made, the pressure on the assembly tool, the speed of work, and time away from the job. Reasonable productivity standards have been established. We are proud to say that, with a younger work force, these standards keep going up, and the incentive pay of employees who exceed standards is rising proportionately.

Our work units are divided into teams. The best motivator to work hard is the high standards of one's peers. Teams, not individuals, earn prizes and bonuses. Winning teams have the satisfaction of knowing they are doing more than their share. Computer screens abound with productivity updates, encouraging employees to note where their teams stand and how productive individuals have been for the hour, week, and month. Computers send congratulatory messages such as "you are working 10% faster than the norm" or messages of concern such as "you are lowering the team average."

Community morale

There is no community without honesty. Any community must take reasonable precautions to protect itself from dishonesty. Just as we inspect the briefcases and purses of visitors exiting our R&D division, the company reserves the right to call up and inspect without notice all data files and observe work-in-progress currently displayed on employees' screens. One random search discovered an employee using the company computer to send out a curriculum vitae seeking employment elsewhere. In another, an employee was running a football pool.

Some companies try to prevent private phone calls on company time by invading their employees' privacy. At DS, encroachments on employees' privacy are obviated by telecommunications programs that block inappropriate numbers (dial-a-joke, dial-a-prayer) and unwanted incoming calls. In addition, an exact record of all dialing behavior is recorded, as is the number from which calls are received. We want our employees to feel protected against any invalid claims against them.

Video and audio surveillance too protects employees from intruders in hallways, parking lots, lounges, and work areas. Vigilance is invaluable in protecting our community from illegal behavior or actions that violate our safety and high commitment to excellence. All employees, including managers, check in and out of various workstations—including the parking lot, main entrance, elevator, floors, office, and even the bathroom—by means of an electronic entry card. In one case, this surveillance probably saved the life of an employee who had a heart attack in the parking lot: when he failed to check into the next workstation after five minutes, security personnel were sent to investigate.

Beyond isolation

Our program takes advantage of the most advanced telecommunications equipment to bind employees to one another and to the company. DS vehicles are equipped with on-board computers using satellite transponders. This offers a tracking service and additional two-way communication. It helps our customers keep inventories down and helps prevent hijacking, car theft, and improper use of the vehicles. Drivers save time since engines are checked electronically. They also drive more safely, and vehicles are better maintained since speed, gear shifts, and idling time are measured.

In addition to locator and paging devices, all managers are given fax machines and personal computers for their homes. These are connected at all times. Cellular telephones are provided to selected employees who commute for more than half an hour or for use while traveling.

Instant communication is vital in today's international economy. The global market does not function only from 9 to 5. Modern technology can greatly increase productivity by ensuring instant access and communication. Periodic disruptions to vacations or sleep are a small price to pay for the tremendous gains to be won in worldwide competition. DS employees share in these gains.

Great companies have always unleashed the power of new technology for the social welfare, even in the face of criticism. During the first industrial revolution, such beloved novelists as Charles Dickens sincerely opposed the strictures of mass production. In time, however, most of the employees who benefited from the wealth created by new factories and machines came to take progress for granted and preferred the modern factory to traditional craft methods. Today we are living through a Second Industrial Revolution, driven by the computer.

Advanced work-support technology is democratic, effective, and anti-hierarchical. DS's balance sheet and the long waiting list of prospective employees indicate how the new program has helped everybody win. To recall the phrase of journalist Lincoln Steffens, "We have been over into the future, and it works." We are a company of the twenty-first century.

HBR's cases are derived from the experiences of real companies and real people. As written, they are hypothetical, and the names used are fictitious.

Dominion-Swann Industries wants its employees to be productive, happy, and safe. Are they?

Four experts on technology and human resource management discuss Dominion-Swann's work-support technology.

JOSEPH MODEROW *is senior vice president and general counsel of United Parcel Service. He also serves on UPS's Technology Steering Committee.*

Nothing is wrong with Dominion-Swann's admirable goals except their priority.

Like many companies, Dominion-Swann seeks to protect and maximize two vital resources critical to its ongoing success: the vast investment of the company in technology and its employees. Nothing is wrong with these admirable goals except their priority. People come second at DS, even in the handbook title which points to technology as the hope for industry and the centerpiece of Dominion-Swann's new workplace.

DS management informs employees that necessary changes in the work environment have been instituted and justifies these changes with a trail of failures rather than a vision of success. But it lacks the curiosity—not to mention wisdom—to explore the causes of its workers' demoralized state.

Despite DS's disturbing actions, competitive companies do have the right to determine, direct, and even measure how employees perform their responsibilities. Anyone who has seen recent UPS commercials will likely identify us with the phrase "We run the tightest ship in the shipping business." When you observe the urgency and determination of our delivery drivers, you may be led to believe that we achieved such efficiency through a corporate culture like that of DS. That is not the case. UPS succeeds because of its conviction that control and efficiency must not be achieved at the cost of employee commitment.

Much of UPS's success is attributable to continuous effort to optimize the efficient use and allocation of people, facilities, equipment, and technology. We do utilize work measurement programs in which drivers are given specific quantitative goals to achieve. This is a valuable tool in properly allocating resources and reflects the fundamental philosophy of "A fair day's wage for a fair day's work." This scientific management is, however, balanced by our commitment to communications programs that allow for an open exchange with employees on matters affecting the work environment, including direct participation in forming and applying company policies.

The DS handbook is not the basic product of managers addressing the needs of the employees they work with; it is primarily the product of a consulting firm charged with developing a "radical restructuring of the work environment." This clinical work follows a well-organized but unjustified pattern. Each instituted change is preceded by an explanation intended to gain employees' understanding and consensus on the action taken. Theft is a problem; therefore the solution is employee monitoring. Poor attitudes have adversely affected production; therefore scents, music, and subliminal messages will alter the workers' perspective of the work environment. Closer scrutiny of any of the justifications reveals obvious self-serving motives for the imposed practices that undermine Dominion-Swann's credibility.

There are three underlying themes in the handbook that undermine its long-term viability as a workable tool to affect employee attitudes and conduct positively.

1. The handbook attempts to establish a model whereby existing and future employees will fit neatly into a "scientifically" developed mold. The baseline of this mold is the "physiological, psychological, social, and demographic factors" of DS's *best* employees, as determined by SciexPlan's expert INDUCT system. Such standardization does not allow sufficient latitude for a diverse work force where creativity can flourish. Corporate mavericks—not corporate clones—bring vitality and diversity to managerial work.

2. The scope of the handbook is particularly disturbing. There seems to be no limit to the areas of an employee's life that are not invaded by personnel practices. On the job, there is continuous monitoring and surveillance of virtually every movement. The camera watches even in the lounge. Leaving work does not provide the refuge of privacy either. Employees are required to be "connected at all times" to the company through the umbilical cord of paging devices, fax machines, and personal computer modems. Disruptions of vacations and sleep become part of the norm in the company's quest for competitive gain. With ever-tightening standards of performance and personal conduct, both on and off the job, a diminishing portion of employees will be able to "measure up," resulting in eroding morale and, probably, open challenges to the strict employment practices and rules.

3. Finally, and most troubling, is the removal of the human element of management and evaluation. This principle is clearly enunciated in the handbook, which establishes that "technical, hardware-based solutions are preferable to supervision and persuasion." It goes on to conclude that "machines are fairer than managers." While we must admit to a computer's edge in accuracy, can we accept that machines make fairer evaluations of people than people do? I think not.

In the final analysis, we are all human and make mistakes, especially when measured with unrelenting scrutiny against the strictest of standards. Under such conditions, I want someone managing me who shares some of my own human frailties and imperfections. A machine suffers only mechanical failures but lacks the spark of human imagination.

Dominion-Swann already exists. Some elements of its organizational strategy have been practiced for over 100 years.

SHOSHANA ZUBOFF *is associate professor at the Harvard Business School and author of* In the Age of the Smart Machine: The Future of Work and Power *(Basic Books, 1988).*

The future creeps in on small feet. Change in the contours of lives and things is incremental and fragmented. We do not awaken suddenly to a brave new world. Ten years ago, our lives *were* different—no PCs, no fax machines. But even as these inventions and the uses we put them to renovate our world, we continue to wake up in the same beds, drive the same routes to work, and look forward to turkey on Thanksgiving. In consequence, the future gets away with a lot, making itself at home in our lives before we've had a chance to say no thank you.

Dominion-Swann Industries sounds like a futuristic workplace, where life is saturated with computers that measure everything from your productivity to your heartbeat, where dreams of a perfectly ordered, clockwork world, shorn of human conflict, can come true. But DS already exists. Its technology strategy is widely adhered to. Some elements of its organizational strategy have been practiced for over 100 years. Others have been implemented and perfected throughout the 1980s.

Dominion-Swann of 1995 rose from the ashes of its managers. Somehow, its managers had lost their authority. There appears to have been, in the late 1980s, a rupture in their relationship with the work force. This was probably because maintaining constructive relationships with workers is demanding. It requires the kind of face-to-face interaction that builds trust, shared values, and reciprocity.

The failure of authority at DS is clear from the symptoms that have made it into the official history—and note that it is the symptoms that were reported, not their causes. Thus we are told about falling levels of productivity, quality, and morale. Employee turnover was on the rise, as were accidents, theft, drug use, and "unseemly behavior."

What to do when authority fails? How do those in power ensure that their commands will be obeyed if they detect that others may doubt their right to leadership? What good is a command if no one takes it seriously? Let's look at the options DS management faced back in 1990. It could have thrown in the towel, liquidated its assets, been taken over. Or it could have chosen to renew and reinvigorate management's authority by creating a workplace based on a new sharing of knowledge and power, where people are entrusted to do the work they know best, and managers are educators, guiding the development of value creation. It could have shown some faith in human beings, could have striven for growth and learning in every employee. It could have demonstrated its belief in the enterprise of management and in the skills and untapped wisdom of the managerial group.

In 1990, there was a growing number of corporate models for such an approach, as many businesses throughout the United States, Europe, and Japan achieved unprecedented economic success pioneering new, more progressive and humane forms of organization—setting new standards for quality, service, and the development of human potential. We will never know why DS leaders chose not to take this approach, but we can guess. Such an approach takes leaders who confront problems when they see them, who believe that human ingenuity and integrity, combined with technical prowess, are our last, best hope for sustained competitiveness.

Instead, DS managers decided that the key to renewal lay in information technology and in so doing tapped into an ancient response to the age-old problem of failed leadership. DS's managers, like other rulers before them, established techniques of control as a fail-safe system to guard against the frailties of their uncertain authority. Feudal kings used to take hostages from a noble's family, just in case he might want to raise a fuss over paying taxes. States employ radar traps, in case someone doesn't obey a speed limit. It was for just such a purpose that DS turned to information technology. As their handbook puts it: "Technical hardware-based solutions are preferable to supervision and persuasion." The means are at hand to shape behavior through monitoring, surveillance, and detection without even the slightest managerial effort.

Technology itself is not to blame for this state of affairs. In fact, information technologies, which represent a radical discontinuity in industrial history, could well lead to more reciprocity in the workplace, not less. Earlier generations of machines were designed to do essentially what human bodies could, only faster, more reliably, and at less cost. With machines, work required less human intervention and, overall, fewer human skills. This process has come to be known as automation. The ideal of automation is the self-diagnosing, self-correcting machine system that runs perfectly without human assistance.

Information technology can be used to automate all sorts of work in factories and offices. But unlike other tools of automation, information technology simultaneously registers data about the conversion processes it governs. Take the example of an industrial robot. It looks like a classic piece of automation, but the same microprocessors embedded in the robot that tell it what to do are also registering data about its activities. That slice of the production process is logged in a very precise way, as the robot supplies data on dozens of variables that could never have been defined or measured without it.

Multiply this effect across a highly automated manufacturing process and what you get is not only a complex machine system doing its job *but also an enormous, dynamic, fluid electronic text*, displayed on video screens and in computer printouts, full of numbers, charts, words, and symbols that portray total plant functioning in a way that never existed—indeed, never could have been imagined—before. The same effect is present in the office environment where we see connections being made between transaction systems, communication systems, management information systems, financial systems, customer and supplier systems, EPOS systems, scanner systems, and imaging systems.

As the time frames in which data are collected and presented become more accelerated, as more sectors of data are integrated, and as access to the systems becomes more widely distributed, the business is rendered transparent, as never before, through a dynamic electronic text. Moreover, anybody with the wit to access the data can discern patterns and dynamics, anticipate problems and opportunities, and make connections.

When information technology works to create this new kind of transparency, it is doing far more than automating—it is performing a second function that I call *informating*. The informated business invites the whole work force to think strategically.

All of which brings us back to Dominion-Swann. For the potential of the informated workplace to be fulfilled, two conditions are critical: an organizational strategy that emphasizes learning and a leadership vision that understands how technology and the organization are integrated to generate more participatory approaches to value creation. The informated business redistributes authority, turns managers into educators, and devolves responsibility on those at the front line of the organization to use information quickly and creatively, where and when it counts.

Has DS created transparency? You bet. But transparency of what? For what? The short answer is transparency of human behavior for the purposes of total control. DS has tapped into the technology's informating power: almost every aspect of employee performance and behavior has been translated into and is displayed in the form of electronic data. But it is a transparency that allows unseen senior managers (the few who survived the demise of management) to monitor and control people and processes down to the tiniest detail, to shape behavior by recording everything and detecting all variances.

Does DS represent a brave new world of organizational trends? Ask Jeremy Bentham, who founded the utilitarian movement at the turn of nineteenth century, and also worried about the unproductive and "unseemly" behavior of workers, paupers, and convicts. Bentham conceived the "Panopticon," a polygonal structured prison-factory, consisting of a central tower from which rows of glass-walled cells emanated. With the use of mirrors fixed around the center tower, it was possible for an observer to see into each cell while remaining invisible to the cells' inhabitants. ("Universal transparency" was the term he liked.)

The assurance of permanent visibility, Bentham thought, would elicit "good behavior" from the inmates. The architecture itself was the guarantee of conformity. It promised observation but eliminated any way for workers or convicts to know for sure if they were being watched. In much the same way, DS relies on the certainty of panoptic power. Transparency is achieved, not through the architecture of a building but rather through the architecture of information systems. In DS language, this is "accountability through visibility." All optimum solutions are decided a priori by the few remaining managers. The only real challenges, they think, are to find a docile work force and design systems that will monitor everything.

In the end, the British government refused to build the Panopticon, and paid Bentham off – some £23,000. Dominion-Swann might have done better to pay off SciexPlan, for as history shows, most people will not remain docile for long. In subtle ways, they begin to develop techniques of defense as countermeasures to the techniques of control with which they must contend. For example, those knowledgeable about software will attempt to confound the systems operations in several ways. They may try to block the system's ability to monitor their behavior or attempt to "snow the computer" by finding ways to alter data traveling upward in the organization. Those with fewer computer skills are more likely to practice passive resistance. They will simply ignore what the computer tells them or blame it when their performance is not up to standard.

For others, the pressure of visibility is enough to reorganize behavior at its roots. Their coping strategy is what I call "anticipatory conformity." These employees so want to avoid the embarrassment of being singled out as a source of variance that they will go out of their way to conform to standards rather than risk detection. Don't count on these employees to figure out how to solve a customer's problem or initiate an improvement in the production process. They are simply too fearful to take any risks.

Finally, there is the intimidating rush of "objective" data about their work with which employees cannot argue and which, at times, they do not even understand. An individual's views count for less than the force of truth that shines through all these real-time facts.

Some humility is, of course, necessary for learning. But humiliation will cause people to give up. Don't count on these employees to detect errors or anticipate problems. It's not that they have stopped thinking but rather that they have ceased to value what they think.

Are things at Dominion-Swann as rosy as they seem? We have only the word of DS managers. And, for all we know, the handbook was itself written by consultants.

DS has failed to capitalize on the full potential offered by its investment in automation.

BILL HOWARD *is vice president of information technology at Bechtel Corporation.*

The date on Dominion-Swann's handbook should read 1895, not 1995. Rather than a company of the twenty-first century, DS brings to mind an organization firmly rooted in the first industrial revolution, one that has applied twenty-first century technology to nineteenth century management practice. Computers are used in much the same way as the tools of the late nineteenth and twentieth centuries: to monitor, audit, replace, deskill, and dehumanize staff and supervision, rather than to empower workers and management to realize a quantum leap in productivity.

In its effort to make the company a home to employees, DS has used computers and telecommunications to produce the modern-day equivalent of the company town or the company store. Every move is logged, monitored, and evaluated – even the bathroom at work and the bedroom at home. Privacy and individualism are severely impaired. The company uses technology to tie the employee to the company but fails to use technology to stimulate individuals to greater creativity and productivity.

The entry-level screening and community health programs capitalize on the vast amounts of information in databases around the country and the capabilities of medical monitoring equipment. DS is pushing the limits of society's tolerance for this type of inquiry and information gathering. It appears to be effective for DS, but management should not be surprised when market opportunities are missed and increasing legislative restrictions in this area of inquiry and discrimination start to appear. And, by its careful selection techniques, DS creates a mediocre and homogeneous group of followers. It also misses the opportunity to include the ideas and values of those creative contributors who fall outside the norm.

Teamwork and suggestions by employees for improved performance are encouraged by DS. But my perception of the DS team is more like a swim team made up of individual performers trying for "personal bests" to aggregate the maximum team score rather than the highly successful work team of the 1990s, which operates more like a basketball team made up of skilled performers who improvise together to capitalize on opportunities as they arise. Interaction is more important than the sum of the individual player's actions. A supervisor serves as the coach rather than as the commander.

For Dominion-Swann to fully exploit the potential of the latest advances in work-support technology, I would suggest.

1. Establish a dialogue among the human resource department, the information technology organization,

and representatives of all parts of the company affected by the use of information technology to sort out which systems enhance productivity and which systems or practices should be modified or abandoned because they induce fear or privacy concerns. All new systems should be planned and implemented with employees' involvement.

2. Use information technology to enhance the power of the individual to participate and to contribute his or her ideas to work rather than simply as monitoring tools. Promote interactive discussions and analysis in a team environment with participation of multiple disciplines at various levels of the organization. Develop systems that allow management to serve as coach or mentor rather than critic or enforcer.

3. Use information technology to establish closer links with business partners outside the company. Extend the reach of DS to a broader team concept that includes suppliers and the all-important customer.

4. Design systems to span across functional boundaries so that teams can be organized electronically to solve problems and contribute to productivity.

5. Train, train, train employees in the use of information systems, and use technology to enhance training so that workers and supervisors can fully understand and buy into delivering the full potential offered by the technology.

6. Encourage a new leadership model that is attuned to technology and that recognizes the need to change the organization and processes to match the tools of the twenty-first century. Identify managers who recognize the interdependence of the various business units and operating functions and who can bridge those boundaries to deliver crossfunctional solutions. Automating old processes and functions without taking into account the powerful capability of the new tools assures that the anticipated payback will not be realized.

7. Continue to reward performance of teams rather than individuals, provide technology to key players to eliminate the barriers of time and distance, encourage healthful lifestyles, reduce middle management layers that merely serve as switches and filters, assure that the company strategy continues to be understood at all levels.

8. Fire SciexPlan, Inc.

Some may be impressed with the five-year gains in worker productivity, employee income, and sales. However, in my view, sales, productivity, and performance in all areas must be measured against the best performers in industry to ensure maintaining a competitive position. I believe Dominion-Swann has failed to capitalize on the full potential offered by its investment in automation and will fall behind more enlightened competition in the last half of the 1990s. But it has no way of knowing that. Dominion-Swann is an underachieving organization because it has failed to see the true potential in information technology: to empower workers to deliver competitive solutions that were not possible without the information tools of the Second Industrial Revolution.

Not only are employees rejecting surveillance techniques, but the courts are too.

KAREN NUSSBAUM *is the executive director of 9 to 5, National Association of Working Women, and president of District 925, Service Employees International Union.*

What's wrong with this picture? Dominion-Swann Industries cares about its employees. DS is committed to its employees. Here's how managers show it:

☐ They weed out the old and infirm and those with family problems.

☐ They use highly personal information on employees and their families and friends to keep out those who don't fit the "norm."

☐ They test urine, check fingerprints, run data checks, inspect files, conduct video surveillance, track movements, monitor.

☐ They control minds, control movement, control substances, control association.

Does that sound like love? DS's policies are discriminatory, invasive, and counterproductive. And though few companies implement such an impressive package of organizational and technological measures, all of these policies exist in one form or another in American businesses—with poor results. I will reflect on a few of them.

Weeding the work force. Dominion-Swann's method for upgrading the work force is to screen for imperfections. Justifiable caution becomes an ugly effort to create an Aryan nation of employees when you start to ask questions about parents' health and lifestyle. In any case, advanced-selection processes are a shortsighted way to respond to a diverse work force in a tight labor market. We are entering an era marked by a shortage of skilled workers. Employers need to adapt to the needs of a variety of new workers—workers who are old, handicapped, foreign, female—instead of just culling the "best." Successful employers will learn how to be strengthened by diversity, instead of hiring only in their own image. Besides, it is still *illegal* to discriminate in hiring on the basis of age and handicap, as well as race, sex, and national origin.

Is there a boss under my bed? DS's surveillance, testing, control, and data-check methods keep tabs on employees round-the-clock, cradle-to-grave, and home-to-office. But what's the point? Most of the information is not very useful to the employers, and I've yet to find the worker who *likes* surveillance. Let's take monitoring, for example. A study by the Office of Technology Assessment (aptly titled *Electronic Supervisor*) said this about monitoring: "The knowledge that one's every move is being watched, without an ability to watch the watcher, can create feelings that one's privacy is being invaded and that one is an object under close scrutiny. Being subject to close scrutiny without an ability to confront the observer may mean the

loss of a feeling of autonomy....The employee may feel powerless and exposed under the gaze of electronic monitoring." In a word, fear.

Take the case of the United Airlines reservation clerk who was disciplined for comments she made to a coworker. She was courteous to an obnoxious customer and handled him well – management had no quarrel with her there. But after this three-minute call, which was monitored, she complained to a coworker. Management, listening in, put her on probation for her remark, then sent her to the company psychiatrist when she complained, and ultimately fired her.

An ad for networking software in the March 13, 1989 issue of *PC Week* makes the following claim: "Close-Up LAN brings you a level of control never before possible. It connects PCs on your network giving you the versatility to instantly share screens and keyboards....You decide to look in on Sue's computer screen....Sue won't even know you are there!...All from the comfort of your chair." Another airline employee got into trouble because her monitoring system strictly enforced a 12-minute limit on bathroom breaks. When she went over by 2 minutes, she was disciplined, and ultimately quit in emotional crisis. A data processor in New York told me that her screen periodically flashed "You're not working as fast as the person next to you." A secretary from Florida told me that the thing she found most offensive about her (generally abusive) boss was that he calls up on *his* VDT the work she's doing, while she's doing it. This is "work support"?

Not just workers. The "higher professions" are being hit too. One reporter told me that as she was typing in her story, her computer flashed "I don't like that lead." A surreptitious editor was butting in on a first draft. This kind of thing makes one feel humiliated, harassed, and under the gun. A leading maker of monitoring software programs says, "Monitoring helps employees. It's the only way we can get everything on the permanent record." But I've never met even one highly poised professional who appreciates this kind of "feedback."

Not only are employees rejecting surveillance techniques, but the courts are too. Legal challenges to employer access to databases of personal information are expected to grow. And workers are filing privacy suits against their employers in unprecedented numbers. Between 1984 and 1987, *20 times* as many workplace privacy suits were decided by U.S. courts than in the three years before. Jury verdicts in favor of workers averaged $316,000 – compared with 1979 and 1980 when no workers won compensation.

Why were they doing this anyway? If for no other reason, I'd advise managers not to follow Dominion-Swann's example because their policies are counterproductive. Studies repeatedly show that monitoring and surveillance of employees lead to high levels of stress, and stress-related diseases are now the most common occupational illness for workers under 40, costing U.S. business hundreds of millions of dollars each year. Even if you start with the Wheaties class of employees, as DS has tried to do, after a period of increased productivity, workers will simply burn out.

Monitoring expert Alan Westin of Columbia University describes Federal Express's "people first" approach to office automation, which was supposed to downplay quantitative measures (recorded through monitoring) and elevate nine "quality" elements. However, the manager of customer service in one regional office, in contradiction to the organizational policy, enforced a campaign designed to "get the handle time down!" Before corrective actions raised quality back to where it had been, the staff experienced high rates of physical and psychological ill-health. Incidentally, once these corrective changes were in place, average handle time dropped below its level under the coercive regime.

And DS will be disappointed if its goal is to bring employees closer to management and create a "homey" team. A survey by the Massachusetts Coalition on New Office Technology shows deep alienation among monitored workers.

Corporate culture does need retooling. There are real problems facing employers, but substituting control and fear for supervision and training is not the answer. Dominion-Swann's new policies are the marks of the *failure* of management, not its crowning achievement. I endorse the call for commitment and professionalization of the workplace. To get there, we need education, training, and respect.

Reprint 90209

READ THE FINE PRINT

REPRINTS
Telephone: 617-495-6192
Fax: 617-495-6985

Current and past articles are available, as is an annually updated index. Discounts apply to large-quantity purchases.

Please send orders to HBR Reprints
Harvard Business School
Publishing Division
Boston, MA 02163.

HOW CAN <u>HARVARD BUSINESS REVIEW</u> ARTICLES WORK FOR YOU?

For years, we've printed a microscopically small notice on the editorial credits page of the *Harvard Business Review* alerting our readers to the availability of *HBR* articles.

Now we invite you to take a closer look at some of the many ways you can put this hard-working business tool to work for you.

IN THE CORPORATE CLASSROOM.

There's no more effective, or cost-effective, way to supplement your corporate training programs than in-depth, incisive *HBR* articles.

Affordable and accessible, it's no wonder hundreds of companies and consulting organizations use *HBR* articles as a centerpiece for management training.

IN-BOX INNOVATION.

Where do your company's movers and shakers get their big ideas? Many find the inspiration for innovation in the pages of *HBR*. They then share the wealth and spread the word by distributing *HBR* articles to company colleagues.

IN MARKETING AND SALES SUPPORT.

HBR articles are a substantive leave-behind to your sales calls. And they can add credibility to your direct mail campaigns. They demonstrate that your company is on the leading edge of business thinking.

CREATE CUSTOM ARTICLES.

If you want to pack even greater power in your punch, personalize *HBR* articles with your company's name or logo. And get the added benefit of putting your organization's name before your customers.

AND THERE ARE 500 MORE REASONS IN THE <u>HBR CATALOG</u>.

In all, the *Harvard Business Review Catalog* lists articles on over 500 different subjects. Plus, you'll find books and videos on subjects you need to know.

The catalog is yours for just $8.00. To order *HBR* articles or the *HBR Catalog* (No. 21019), call 617-495-6192. Please mention telephone order code 025A when placing your order. Or FAX us at 617-495-6985.

And start putting *HBR* articles to work for you.

Harvard Business School Publications

Call 617-495-6192 to order the *HBR Catalog*.

(Prices and terms subject to change.)

YOU SAID: AND WE SAID:

❝Give us training tools that are relevant to our business...ones we can use *now*.❞

❝We need new cases that stimulate meaningful discussion.❞

❝It can't be a catalog of canned programs... everything we do is custom.❞

❝Make it a single source for up-to-date materials ...on the most current business topics.❞

❝Better yet if it's from a reputable business school. That adds credibility.❞

Harvard Business School Publications

❝Introducing the Harvard Business School Publications Corporate Training and Development Catalog.❞

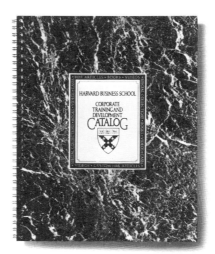

You asked for it. And now it's here.

The Harvard Business School Publications Corporate Training and Development Catalog is created exclusively for those who design and develop custom training programs.

It's filled cover-to-cover with valuable materials you can put to work on the spot. You'll find a comprehensive selection of cases, *Harvard Business Review* articles, videos, books, and more.

Our new catalog covers the critical management topics affecting corporations today, like Leadership, Quality, Global Business, Marketing, and Strategy, to name a few. And it's all organized, indexed, and cross-referenced to make it easy for you to find precisely what you need.

HOW TO ORDER.
To order by FAX, dial 617-495-6985. Or call 617-495-6192. Please mention telephone order code 132A. Or send this coupon with your credit card information to: HBS Publications Corporate Training and Development Catalog, Harvard Business School Publishing Division, Operations Department, Boston, MA 02163. **All orders must be prepaid.**

Order No.	Title	Qty. ×	Price +	Shipping* =	Total
39001	Catalog		$8		

Prices and terms subject to change.
*For orders outside Continental U.S.: 20% for surface delivery. Allow 3-6 months. *Express Deliveries* billed at cost; all foreign orders not designating express delivery will be sent by surface mail.

☐ VISA   ☐ American Express   ☐ MasterCard

Card Number_____ Exp. Date_____

Signature_____

Telephone_____ FAX_____

Name_____

Organization_____

Street_____

City_____ State/Zip_____

Country_____ ☐ Home Address   ☐ Organization Address

Please Reference Telephone Order Code 132A